I Am Nuwaubian

CJ Nelson

CONTENTS

Preface| About the Author

I am a native of the small city of Little Rock, Arkansas. I was raised in a single parent household within the John Barrow Community by an industrious mother who, although could not give me everything I wanted, always found a way to get me the things that I needed, including more love than any child could ever ask for. Like most young "black" boys of my generation, my childhood and adolescent years were fraught with the challenges faced by inner-city kids. I am living proof that if practiced earnestly, Nuwaubu can and will change the direction of your life. I am the proof that people can change and that almost everyone deserves a second chance at life. However, what you choose to do with your second chance rests squarely upon your shoulders. I chose to make the most of my second chance. I chose to stop making excuses for my own ignorance and took upon my shoulders the responsibility of educating myself not only through a college degree but by studying those revolutionaries that blazed the trail upon which I travel.

Today, I am a college graduate with four degrees. I am also a high school dropout with a GED. Those who do not know me personally, often incorrectly assume that the person that I am today, and the path I walked to get her are one in the same. This could not be any further from my actual life experiences. In my early 20s I lived on the streets with my mother. Many nights we slept in the back of her SUV in the parking deck of a hospital in our former neighborhood. I literally owned one pair of clothes, two pairs of shoes, and a broken-down Mazda 626 with a blown transmission. I have walked more than I have owned a vehicle. When I say walk, I literally mean hours at a time to and from work, in the heat, rain, and on a few occasions even in the snow. I have gone weeks at a time surviving off of free coffee from my job, bummed cigarettes, and $1.00 chili at Wendy's once a day. I have worked two and three jobs at a time, for the better half of my working years. All of which is only a fraction of my story.

Exactly, 364 days, 21 hours, and 30 minutes ago I lost my mother in a botched colostomy bag surgery at the very same hospital where we slept in the parking deck. Less than a week prior to her last trip to the hospital she asked me "don't you think that it's about time that you wrote that book." My exact words to her were "I will start working on that book when you get better." She passed away a little over a week later. Sometimes I feel as if I lost my best friend. However, I realize that my mother will never die again. This book is dedicated to her memory.

 May you exist beyond space and time, forever in peace and tranquility!

Ms. Queen Esther Scott

I would be remiss in my duties as a rational human being if I neglected to acknowledge the overwhelming contributions that others, outside of my mother, have played in contributing to the person that I am today. First, I would like to thank Katie Scott! Thank you for always being there for me, my mother, and my children. You are in many respects, my other mother. I love you and I wish you well on your next journey. I would like to thank the entire Scott Family for the decades of love that they poured into me from my earliest childhood years until this very moment. All of my aunts, those that are here with us and those who have transitioned as ancestors. I would like to thank all of my uncles, those that are living and those who have transitioned, especially my Uncle Evans Ray Scott. You and my mother loved each other dearly. It broke my heart to hear that you had passed less than a week after we laid her to rest. I would like to thank my grandmother Gracie L. Scott, for all the times you made me fetch a switch and disciplined me when I messed up, all the times you made me work in the fields plowing, planting, hoeing, and reaping. They say that steel sharpens steel, and you were by far that steel that made the family grow and mature. I would like to thank my great Aunt Sugar for all the love you shared with your sisters' kids and grand kids! I would like to thank Dedra Evans for the love, care, and the prayers that you gave freely to me over the years. Oh, and for the suit! It is still hanging in the closet to this very day. I would like to thank Mr. John Goins who, shortly after I began my career in insurance, took me under his wing and began teaching me about what it means to be an "African American" insurance agent. I would also like to thank Valerie Hernandez, Melvin Wilson, and Raymond Davis. It seems that no matter how far our individual journeys in life take us, we always seem to find our way back home. This list, by far, does not encompass the range of people who contributed to my life experience. However, this list includes those people that made significant contributions to my life and also transitioned in the 12-18 leading up to my mother's passing. I want to personally thank each and every one of you for having a profound impact on my life and may you rest in peace and tranquility. When she was ill and could not attend your memorial services, I did whatever was within my means to ensure that I showed up to pay respects on her behalf and mine.

Further, I would like to thank Charles E. Jones and the entire Jones, Lunon, and Chambliss families. Chuck, we have watched each other grow over the entire course of our lives. Thank you for always being there for me. Thank you for being a loyal friend and cousin. The person that I am today would not exist if it were not for you. The fact that my mother called you just hours before she passed should let you know exactly how she felt about you. Ms. Jackie Porchay and the Porchay family, thank you for putting a pillow under our heads when we were homeless, and for showing me how to make what is now my world-famous cheese dip. To Red, my big head goddaughter, I would like to say congratulations on achieving one of the biggest milestones in life. To many of our younger generation are unable to see the value in a college education. Separate and apart from all of the personal benefits that you will receive, completing this monumental task will inspire your family for years to come. I wish you success on your new journey! Shronica Thomas and the Thomas and Noid families, thank you for being honorable and noble friends. To Kelis "KB" Battles, I have watched you mature into a remarkable young lady. My hope for you is that you continue to thrive, forever striving toward success and that you let nothing, or no one veer you from your path. Monica "MJ" Johnson, I want to thank you for brushing off my rough edges, giving me a chance, and setting my feet on the right path. Who knew that a temporary job, as a clerk, would blossom into a lifelong career in insurance? Dorie Jackson, thank you bro for helping me land that job. My hope for you is that you are in good health and good spirits. Delmarche Patton, thank you for all of the rides, and for keeping me in line. To Sonja and Shakita, thank you for coming to rescue when I was all alone and in despair because I could not be with my family on Thanksgiving! Tell Lexi she better get in there and make some Oodles of Noodles! James Huston, you are my brother, and I love you man. No matter where you are or what's going on, all you need to do is pick up the phone and I got you, bro. Cameron D. White I love you, bro. All you have to do is call. Jamie Washington and Family, thank you for being patient with me. I know that I have been extremely busy over the course of this past year. However, it was imperative that I get this book out now. Jamie, I would also like to thank you for listening all the time I called you to vent and for talking some sense into me whenever I am tripping. You are a phenomenal businesswomen, mother, and person. A true leader in the community! Ryan Turner, Stanley Saladin, Ricky Farley, Gerren Lacy, Christopher Williams, Robert Thomas, and Curtis Bell and their families, I love you brothers, and I appreciate all the times you have come through for me in the clutch. People on the outside will never know what it's all about and I am cool with that. To Wayne A. Oliver, Marcus Kinnard-Bing, Kary Green, Marshall Vance, Dr. David D. Colter, and Sigma Gamma Lambda, I am grateful to have met you brothers and although it's a struggle at times I have no intentions on taking any backward steps as I wouldn't dream of letting you down. It's my time to follow my wife, as she followed me when I needed her most. I am making my way back; I just need a little more time. To the entire John Barrow Community, it's all Love! I would never forget or turn my back on my home! You forced me to grow up and for that I am forever grateful. To my siblings, LaShundra, Dwight, Nichol, and April, I love you and I am grateful to have you as a part of my life. Regardless of where our individual journeys take us in life, I will always do everything within my power to be there when you need me. Uncle Dennis Nelson, I love you man. May you rest in peace and tranquility. All of my uncles and aunts, cousins and extended family collectively "The Nelson Clan" I love you all and thank you for always believing in me. To the entire Scott, Smith, Everette, Taylor and extended families I want to thank you for all of the love that you have poured into me over the years. Although it may have taken some time to kick in, all of the lessons and guidance have carried me through the roughest times of my life. To my father, Mr. Vernon Nelson, I love you and thank you for being a part of my life. I cannot forget Joanne, thank you for keeping my "Wxyz" (Wise aka Pops) in line.

Last, but definitely not least, I would like to thank Kori T. Nel- son, Zion D. Rochez, Ralynn C. Rand, and Latrisha M. Nel- son. To my Big Baby Girl Lynn, I love you. I know that you have your own life to live, and I respect that. You are a beautiful and intelligent young lady and now is your time to thrive. There is absolutely nothing that you cannot do, there is no where you cannot go, there is nothing that you cannot aspire to be. Continue to strive toward greatness, let nothing hold you back, and most importantly make sure that you are not standing in your own way. Zion D. Rochez, you and that video game drive me crazy at times, but I love you little man and I want the best for you. I know you may think I am hard on you at time, and I am, but because I care. I care about your safety, well-being, and most of all your future. My hope is that one day when you are older and you look back over your life, you realize exactly how much. To my baby girl, Kori thank you for being my reason. I love you and I fight against the world every day for you. One of my greatest fears is that I would be foolish enough to do anything that would jeopardize your well-being or your future. To my wife, La-trisha M. Nelson, thank you for being there when I needed you most. I could never really express how much that meant to me. Aside from be-ing extremely pretty, you are a beautiful soul. I love you and I will always consider your well-being and the well-being of our family before mak-ing any moves.

I Am Nuwaubian

I Am Nuwaubian

The prevailing opinion among scientists today is that race has no scientific significance and operates purely as a social construct created to establish and justify systems of power, privilege, and oppression. While a person's skin color may be superficial and possess no scientific value, race (as in racial identity) and skin color are altogether two separate notions. The simple truth of the matter is that the term "race," as in skin color, is insufficient at describing the components that constitute a shared racial identity, or ethnicity, as a more appropriate choice of words. Ethnicity is a term used to describe how others perceive us and how we perceive ourselves in respect to a shared racial identity. Ethnicity specifically refers to one's ethnic traits which may include skin tone or texture, character, culture, background, religion, language, association, or affiliations.

To be Nuwaubian, as referenced within the context of our discussions, is to be part of an ethnic group that proudly identifies with the distinct heritage of Africans in America. Today, we seek to reclaim and redefine our ethnic and cultural identities. To be Nuwaubian is to consciously acknowledge our affiliation with a set of shared experiences, struggles, and triumphs that are rooted in the African diaspora and profoundly influenced by the American socio-cultural landscape. Nuwaubian, as an identity, not only recognizes our past but actively engages our present, as we continuously navigate and shape our collective future. It involves embracing our unique cultural practices, traditions, and values while also advocating for our rights and visibility within the broader societal framework of American society. In essence, being Nuwaubian is a dynamic and evolving expression of our heritage and enduring quest for self-definition and empowerment in a complex and diverse world.

Being Nuwaubian transcends the mere physical traits that might connect an individual to the continent of Africa. It involves a profound recognition of our unique history as the American descendants of African slaves, our fused African and America cultural practices, peculiar values, and strong communal bonds. This identity requires acknowledging the persistent impact of systemic challenges and historical adversities while also celebrating the resilience, creativity, and enduring spirit of our community. Nuwaubians often engage with traditions and customs that honor our ancestral legacies; yet reflect contemporary expressions of identity influenced by a Eurocentric American society. This engagement manifests itself through many unique forms of language, spirituality, social norms, and artistic endeavors that define the Nuwaubian narrative.

Further, Nuwaubu and being Nuwaubian is an ongoing process of learning and evolution. Our identities, inherently fluid, resist static definitions, reflecting the dynamic nature of our existence. In fact, they actively respond to the evolving socio-cultural dynamic. This vivacity extends beyond personal identity, encompassing cultural and ethnic dimensions, which must continuously evolve to maintain their significance within the broader tapestry of American history and ensure that our collective identity remains vibrant and relevant. To be Nuwaubian is to embody a unique collective identity, intricately woven into the fabric of America, which acknowledges our historical roots while actively shaping a future where our identity is understood, respected, and celebrated on its own terms. This treble engagement with past, present, and future encapsulates the essence of being Nuwaubian, underscoring our commitment to preserving heritage while simultaneously charting a path forward.

What is Nuwaubu?

Before we can begin to overstand exactly who Nuwaubians are, we must first develop an overstanding of this thing we call Nuwaubu. Over the years I have watched many "Nuwaubians" (to use the term loosely) promote various religious doctrines and dogma, false "facts," fanciful tales, and stake outright outlandish claims of "Black" superiority all under the premise of Nuwaubu. Yet in all of our "black" superiority we have allowed ourselves to be robbed of not only our material possessions but even our freedom, identity, and history. Fortunately, Rev. Malachi Z. York provided us with a clear and precise definition of the term Nuwaubu. According to his book entitled "What is Nuwaubu?" York defines Nuwaubu as the Science of Sound Right Reason and explains that Sound Right Reasoning is achieved through Right Knowledge, Right Wisdom, and Right Overstanding (York n.d.).

Thus, Nuwaubu is a philosophical science, rooted in the principles of Sound Right Reason. Sound Right Reason, within the context of Nuwaubu, refers to a very specific, systematic approach to thinking that emphasizes the importance of complete and accurate information (Right Knowledge), wisdom in the application of that knowledge (Right Wisdom), and a level of comprehension beyond a basic understanding (Right Overstanding) as the foundational elements for personal development. Unlike religious frameworks, Nuwaubu prioritizes a scientific approach to understanding reality. It encourages its adherents to seek empirical evidence in order to establish a rational consistency in their beliefs and world views. At its core, Nuwaubu serves as the guiding principle for interpreting the world and making informed decisions. This principle not only requires a thorough comprehension of factual information but also demands a critical evaluation of that evidence and its implications.

The principles of Sound Right Reason dictate Right Knowledge as the foundation of all understanding. Right knowledge, within the context of Nuwaubu, is accurate and verifiable information obtained through objective in-depth study and based on scientific fact, ensuring that decisions are made on a solid foundation of truth. Sound Right Reason also emphasizes the importance of wisdom in the application of knowledge. Right Wisdom dictates ethical decision making that considers the long-term consequences of our actions and the welfare of all humanity. In the Science of Nuwaubu, the integration of wisdom and knowledge is essential for navigating the complexities of modern life, highlighting the system's holistic approach to personal and societal development. Right Overstanding represents a deeper level of comprehension above that of a basic understanding. It includes inferential comprehension, allowing individuals to draw logical conclusions from observed or recalled information.

When correctly applied, Nuwaubu challenges individuals to engage in reflective thinking to ensure that their perceptions are aligned with objective reality. This alignment promotes a clearer understanding of both self and the universe, reinforcing the importance of reasoned analysis in all aspects of life. Moreover, Nuwaubu's emphasis on right wisdom extends to a holistic view of existence, where the interconnectedness of all objects that exist within time and space is realized, thereby fostering a profound sense of awareness and insight. In this framework, the pursuit of wisdom is not merely an abstract ideal but a practical endeavor that shapes ethical decision-making and responsible actions.

The culture of Nuwaubu incorporates a deep commitment to our African lineage. It encourages Nuwaubians to embrace their African heritage while actively participating in the forging of a future where our collective ethnic identity is both respected and celebrated. It highlights the importance of maintaining cultural relevance in an ever-changing world. Nuwaubu draws on the historical and spiritual traditions of the Ancient Nile River Valley and other African civilizations. It also serves as a cultural identity for people of color here in the Americas, particularly those who identify as descendants of Africa slaves and who seek to reclaim and redefine their ethnic and cultural identities.

Nuwaubu is not a set of beliefs, but rather a dynamic and practical approach to reasoning that transcends the boundaries of religion and emphasizes continuous learning and adaptation based on objective fact. It offers a framework for understanding the world based on empirical knowledge and sagacious judgement. Although it is squarely rooted in African tradition, its commitment is to better the human experience and guiding individuals toward informed decision-making and a keen awareness of their place in the world.

3

What is Right Knowledge?

The initial step toward Sound Right Reasoning within the system of Nuwaubu is acquiring Right Knowledge. The American Heritage Dictionary defines knowledge as a state of familiarity, awareness, or understanding gained through experience or study. Right Knowledge, then, may be defined as a state of knowledge obtained through the in-depth study of accurate and complete scientific facts and information. Right Knowledge is exact, objective, and always based on verifiable facts! This much is true regardless of our inability to comprehend or reconcile such knowledge with our current system of values or beliefs.

We may accept an argument as truth because it aligns with our individual experiences and beliefs, or it is supported by a substantial body of evidence and through a process of logic and reasoning we have determined it to be true. However, it does not necessarily follow that because an argument aligns with our individual experiences or beliefs, is supported by a body of evidence, and results from logical reasoning that an argument is in fact, true. As human beings we have the tendency to seek out, interpret, recall, and favor information that reaffirms, and thus reinforces our current beliefs and values. Nevertheless, we will not elucidate any further on this tendency, known as Confirmation Bias, as it is outside of the scope of this particular chapter. We will, however, approach this topic during a later chapter. For now, we only require a basic understanding of Confirmation Bias to illustrate how it works to distort reality and undermine decision making.

For the moment, let us consider the circumstances surrounding the 2020 U.S. general election. During the months leading up to election day, then incumbent president Donald J. Trump and his allies, began laying the foundation for a 'Big Lie' propaganda technique[1] that would eventually become known as the 'Stop the Steal' movement to overturn the 2020 U.S. Presidential election should Democratic nominee Joseph R. Biden emerge as President Elect (Homans 2022). As early as August, at least a full 3 months prior to the general election, Trump can be found on the campaign trail suggesting that "The only way we're going to lose this election is if the election is rigged!". He criticized vote-by-mail and absentee ballots as propitious to election fraud. Donald Trump continued asserting allegations of wide-spread voter fraud during the days leading up to and following the election. Then, on November 7th, as Joe Biden's lead became more apparent, Donald Trump tweeted "I WON THIS ELECTION, BY A LOT!" Trump vowed to take legal action, exclaiming "this election is far from over!"

By the time Certificates of Ascertainment from the several states had reached the joint session of congress on January 6th, 2021, thousands of Trumps supported had gathered outside of the National Mall in Washington D.C. and conspired to storm the United States Capital to prevent the certification and subsequent installation of Joseph R. Biden as the 46th president of the United States of America. Notwithstanding the fact that in September of 2020, just months prior to the general election, then FBI Director Christopher A. Wray (a Donald Trump appointee) testified under oath before the United States Congress that the FBI had "not see any kind of coordinated national voter fraud effort in a major election, whether by mail or otherwise."

Following the 2020 general elections, the Trump Campaign initiated more than fifty individual lawsuits in several key battleground states around the country. All but three of these cases have since been dismissed, withdrawn, or dispositioned against the former president as dozens of courts at both the federal and state level have rejected Trumps claims of widespread voter fraud in the 2020 U.S. Presidential election. Donald Trump is currently awaiting trial on four separate criminal cases, including one forty-one count indictment for alleged election interference in the State of Georgia.

Despite insurmountable evidence to the contrary, some 30% of Americans and 70% of Republican or Republican leaning respondents still believe that President Biden's 2020 Election Victory was illegitimate (Kamisar 2023). Our question, then becomes, how could millions of Americans fall for the 'Big Lie'? In our search to uncover the underlying cause of such conspiratorial gullibility we need only focus our attention on the human tendency to seek out, interpret, favor, and recall information in such a way that reinforces and support our current belief and values.

The circumstances surrounding, and consequences resulting from the 'Big Lie' and the 'Stop the Steal' movements underscore the importance of ensuring that the information upon which we base our decisions is factual. Without accurate and complete facts (Right Knowledge), one cannot expect to engage in sound reasoning. To remain abreast of current events, formulate an accurate view of society, and resolve the ever-growing list of global issues we must always remain diligent in our search for relevant and objective facts.

Evidence supports facts by providing a basis for their validation through logical reasoning, empirical observation, and other forms of verification. Evidence is crucial for establishing Right Knowledge. There are six broad categories of evidence that serve as the foundation of our understanding and inform our decision-making process:

Personal Experience

Personal Experience may be defined as an "active participation in events or activities, leading to the accumulation of knowledge or skill (Farlex,

Inc. n.d.). This firsthand experience can, at times, verify the truth of certain statements or facts. However, relying solely on personal experience has its limitations. It may not be practical nor possible in every situation, especially when dealing with complex issues or events beyond our immediate environment. Additionally, personal biases and perceptions can affect how we interpret these experiences, making it essential to corroborate personal insights with other types of evidence for a more comprehensive understanding.

Anecdotal Evidence

Anecdotal Evidence is based only on personal observation, collected in a casual or non-systematic manner. If accurate and honest, anecdotal evidence corroborates and substantiates truth. There are obvious limitations to anecdotal evidence. Perception, perspective, recollection, and bias all diminish the reliability of anecdotal evidence. In the United States we rely on anecdotal evidence (witness testimony) in courts of law and equity. It is important to point out the fact that in a court of law, witness testimony can be used by both the prosecution and the defense through the process of cross examination. This process highlights the need for careful scrutiny, as anecdotal evidence alone may not provide a complete or objective picture.

Expert Opinions

Expert Opinion (also known as an Appeal to Authority) is a type of evidence in which an influential figure (such as an experienced professional or expert) provides a professional commentary to support a particular position. While valuable, it is obvious that this type of evidence has its own set of limitations. It is essential to cite credible sources, showing that your arguments are supported by prior analysis, research, case studies, laws, and regulations. However, insisting that a claim is true simply be- because it favored by an authority or expert, without any other supporting evidence is fallacy. Thus, it is crucial to combine expert opinions with other types of evidence to authenticate knowledge and build a well- rounded, credible argument.

Research Studies

Research or Case Studies involve intensive and highly detailed investigation and analysis of individuals, groups, scenarios, subjects, or states of existence to uncover facts or principles about a subject, pattern, or phenomenon. Case studies are oft used to advance knowledge and expertise in a particular field of study and promote critical thinking and analytical discussion. Using the Scientific Method, researchers construct or evaluate a hypothesis, analyze data, draw conclusions, communicate results, and establish substantive facts. Research studies may be time consuming and difficult to replicate. In the absence of appropriate controls, research studies may also be influenced by personal bias and emotion, underscoring the importance of rigorous methodology to ensure reliable and valid findings.

Demonstrative Evidence

Demonstrative Evidence refers to evidence that is used to help illustrate or clarify testimony or facts presented in a case. This type of evidence can include diagrams, models, simulations, charts, and other visual aids that help make complex information easily comprehensible. Although it is not evidence in itself, it is used to support or explain arguments or other forms of evidence. Demonstrative evidence can make abstract or detailed information more tangible! While useful for clarifying complex information, demonstrative evidence has several limitations. It can be subjective and open to different interpretations, and its accuracy depends on precise construction. Simplification can lead to the omission of vital details, and potential bias in creation can skew the evidence. Manipulation is possible, presenting information in a way that supports a particular narrative. Additionally, the effectiveness of demonstrative evidence depends on the audience's ability to understand it correctly, which can vary.

Intuition

Intuition is the faculty of instinctively knowing or comprehending a thing without the use of conscious reasoning, proof, or acute insight. While intuition can guide decision-making, it is limited as a form of evidence because it is subjective and cannot be objectively studied or measured by others. This subjectivity makes it relevant only to the individual experiencing intuition. Relying solely on intuition in arguments can be problematic and should be supplemented with more objective evidence to strengthen its claims and ensure a comprehensive understanding of the topic.

The journey toward Sound Right Reason within the system of Nuwaubu begins with acquiring Right Knowledge, which relies on accurate, objective, and verifiable facts. It is crucial that we diligently verify the knowledge and information that we encounter, discarding falsehoods and accepting truth, using the wisdom of these six broad categories of evidence. Each category has its strengths and limitations, emphasizing the need for a comprehensive approach in authenticating information. By critically examining and corroborating evidence from these categories, we can navigate complex issues more effectively, ensuring our decisions are based on sound reasoning and true overstanding.

[1] For more information on the 'Big Lie' propaganda technique please review the "Big Lie" Exposed: A Rhetorical Analysis of Nazi-German in 22 Lessons https://www.hoover.org/news/big-lie-exposed-rhetorical-analysis-nazi-german-22-lessons

4 |

What is Right Wisdom?

The second step toward Sound Right Reason in the system of Nuwaubu is Right Wisdom. Today there exists no universally accepted general definition of wisdom. Most modern definitions emphasize cognition, cleverness, life experience, and a concern for the welfare of humanity as prerequisites of wisdom. The Oxford Dictionary defines wisdom as the quality of being wise, having experience, knowledge, and good judgement. Wisdom may present itself in the form of wise actions or wise thinking. In the system of Nuwaubu, Right Wisdom involves applying the appropriate interpretation to the correct set of facts in an effort to develop a comprehensive overstanding of a thing.

Knowledge vs. Wisdom

Knowledge and wisdom are two similar but altogether distinct notions. Knowledge, as previously defined, is a state of familiarity, awareness, or understanding gained through first-hand experience or acquaintance with relevant facts and information. Conversely, wisdom encompasses the capacity to aptly apply knowledge in making thoughtful and beneficial decisions in various aspects of life. Wisdom relates to good judgement, decision making, and choices based on intellectual capacity and experience. It often requires an overstanding of the broader context and implications of knowledge, as well as the ability to consider the long-term consequences of our actions. We use wisdom to navigate complex situations, solve problems, and make ethical decisions.

Knowledge alone has proven itself incapable of effectively addressing society's most pressing issues. The absence of wisdom, especially in those in positions of power, has resulted in some of history's most devastating calamities. For the moment, let us consider the development of the first atomic bomb. In August of 1942, then President Franklin D. Roosevelt commissioned the formation of the Manhattan Engineering District, aimed at developing a functional nuclear fission-based weapon. J. Robert Oppenheimer, a theoretical physicist and professor of physics at the University of California at Berkley was charged with leading this effort. On July 16, 1945, at 5:29 a.m., Oppenheimer and a team of two hundred scientist, soldiers, and technicians successfully detonated a 13-pound plutonium test bomb named Trinity in the Chihuahuan Desert of Alamogordo, New Mexico. The result, 140,000 killed in Hiroshima, 70,000 killed in Nagasaki, and countless lives lost as a result of nuclear radiation. In less than a century following the successful detonation of the first atomic bomb humanity has had to endure the Cold War, The Kyshtym Nuclear Disaster, The Cuban Nuclear Crisis, Chernobyl, and a world that today inches closer to a nuclear Third World War. The scientists and engineers involved in the research responsible for the world's first nuclear weapons possessed immense knowledge in the domains of nuclear physics, atomic theory, chemistry, and mathematics. However, had wisdom dominated their research we might live in a world free of nuclear strife.

Human intelligence has increased substantially over the past century with differences ranging from three to five IQ points per decade. This phenomenon, known as the "Flynn effect," refers to the observed long-term increase in intelligence test scores measured across many parts of the world throughout the 20th century (Samuelson 2023). It's important to note that the Flynn effect does not necessarily imply that people are becoming innately more intelligent over time, but rather that changes in environment, education, and societal factors are contributing to better performance on intelligence tests. Today, we live in an

America more xenophobic, more divided, and closer societal collapse than at any other time since the American Civil War. Like any other period in American history beset with peril we need leaders and a population that can make wise decisions as they take direct action.

Cognitive Components of Wisdom

Integrating a multicultural perspective is vital to developing a comprehensive awareness of this abstraction that we call wisdom. Our personal values and world views, both of which are influenced by culture, play a pivotal role in developing our conception of this notion of wisdom. Thus, the elements that constitute wisdom (wise actions or wise thinking) may vary from culture to culture. Our question then becomes, what elements constitute wisdom consistently across various cultures?

As a behavior (wise actions), wisdom is commonly associated with constructive actions in which a well-motivated individual draws on cleverness and creativity to develop effective solutions that mitigate adverse effects for all stakeholders. As a psychological trait (wise thinking), wisdom combines virtue and cleverness, drawing on intelligence, knowledge, and experience, all of which are developed through continuous practice.

Cognition

Cognition is the term used to describe the mental processes involved in gaining knowledge and cultivating comprehension. At its essence, cognition is the process of thinking and learning. As human beings, our cognitive processes also include knowing, remembering, judging, and problem-solving, among others. Cognitive Psychology is the field of psychology that studies how people think, and the processes involved in cognition. Although Western Civilization credits early Greek philosophers, namely Plato and Aristotle, with establishing the field of Cognitive Psychology, it likely dates back to Hieratic Scrolls of Hermes and the Pyrophyte's Order of the Khemetic Mysteries[1]. Khemetic Hierophants, Pyrophytes, and Neophytes were strict adherents to Ma'at, or what Greeks later referred to as virtue! A lack of consideration for the Principles of Ma'at, or a lack of virtue, is what has allowed the western world to not only murder and kill to get their hands on the wealth of Africa, but to also use that wealth[2] to commit the worst atrocities humanity has ever witnessed.

Virtue

Giving the vast expanse of knowledge and information circulating throughout society, and its apparent inability to effectively address today's most pressing global issues, it is evident that there must exist some quality beyond intelligence that is essential in shaping wise thoughts and wise actions. American Psychologist and Psychometrician Robert J. Sternberg rightly suggested that "morality and ethics are integral to wisdom." What Mr. Sternberg and the rest of western civilization are now realizing, and what Africans knew millennia ago, is that only through virtue (Ma'at) can we ensure that in complex situations, our actions at a minimum sustain and at their best improve, the collective wellbeing of humanity. The Greek concept of Virtue (ARETE) is but a haphazard imitation of Ma'at, which was violated upon Alexander III of Macedon's violent entry into the grand lodges at Heliopolis, Memphis, and Thebes. This singular act ensured that western civilization would never truly overstand the concept of Ma'at (Truth, Justice, Harmony, Balance, Order, Reciprocity, and Propriety), the purpose of existence, nor "The Mysteries" of Ancient Khemet. It also ensured that this ancient pedagogy of wisdom would be all but lost to humanity as a result of the solemn oath (under the penalty of death) undertaking by all initiates of the brotherhood.

Aristotle was profane(uninitiated) to the ancient brotherhood and as such he was unaware of the systems installed to safeguard the wealth of Ancient Khemet. Incapable of deciphering the sacred carvings (hieroglyphs, Tongue of the Gods), the Greek Rulers of "Egypt" resorted to force to extract this knowledge from what remained of the fragmented brotherhood (The British Museum 2017). Unlike the Athenians who had executed Socrates and persecuted Plato for discussing this strange foreign religion, Greeks had always been attracted by lure of the mysterious Nile River Valley civilizations. Alexander himself had been a student of Aristotle! His father, Philip II of Macedonia, hired Aristotle as a private tutor for an adolescent Alexander. As a student of Aristotle, he would have undoubtedly been exposed to what little Aristotle knew of "The Mysteries" by way of his teacher Plato, and Plato's teacher Socrates who is suspected of having been duly initiated into brotherhood. This would explain why Socrates refused to flee after having been condemned to death for impiety (practicing foreign religions, namely the Mysteries of Egypt from which Philosophy is derived) and corrupting the youth (teaching his students this foreign doctrine). Alexander III would go on to fulfill his father's ambitions of conquering Africa and Asia.

According to ancient Greek Philosophers, the concept of virtue (ARETE) is tied to the notion of function (ERGON). Virtue disregards morality and concerns only the excellent performance of function. Therefore, the virtues of a thing are those that enable it to perform excellently, its proper function, function being that which it performs exceptionally well (Haslanger n.d.). Thence human virtue, as defined by early Greek philosophers, is that which enables a human being to perform excellently, the proper function (ERGON) of being human. Naturally, the question that follows is, "what are the proper functions of being human?" This simple question presents an insurmountable challenge to the Greek concept of virtue.

While this insular approach to essentiality may suffice for inanimate objects such as a chair, sentient life forms are much more intricate and complex. Let us briefly consider the fundamental nature, or virtue, of a chair which is to serve as a seat. Our question then is what are the virtues of a chair, or what enables a chair to perform excellently as a seat? Naturally, one might suppose that having four legs is prerequisite for being a chair. However, we know that not all chairs have four legs or any legs at all for that matter (as in the case of a bean bag or gamer chair). Therefore, we may conclude that having legs is not a virtue of being a chair. We might also suppose that all chairs have a seat. I cannot say that I have ever encountered a chair without a seat. Therefore, we may conclude that having a seat is essential too, and thus a virtue of being a chair. Do all chairs support objects at rest? The essential nature of a chair is to support objects at rest. Therefore, we may conclude that supporting objects at rest is prerequisite to and a virtue of being a chair. Without going too far down the rabbit hole let us briefly consider what would constitute a human virtue according to the early Greek definition. Again, for early Greek philosophers' virtue (ARETE) is intertwined with the notion of function (ERGON). Function being that which human beings do exceptionally well. Our question then is, what do human beings do exceptionally well? In an attempt to address this seemingly simple question we quickly begin to realize that there exists no definitive answer to the question of what human beings do well[3]. Any answer would be purely subjective and only yield an illiberal response.

Ma'at

What early Greek philosophers sought to understand, is what we know today as ethics. Ma'at, at its core, is but one of the world's oldest standards of ethics. Today, wisdom is often defined as encompassing a concern for the well-being of humanity. Our ancestors recognized that strict adherence to Ma'at was necessary to ensure that our actions, even in the complex situations, would at the very least maintain and at their best enhance the collective welfare of humanity without infringing upon the rights and interests of others.

Morals/Ethics

Contemporary definitions of virtue have since evolved to encompass moral excellence and righteousness. Throughout the remainder of the book, use of the word "virtue" shall refer to modern definitions unless otherwise noted. Having established virtue (moral excellence and righteousness) as a necessary condition of wisdom, let us briefly explore four well known virtues commonly associated with sagacious conduct and wise thinking. Greek philosophy recognized Four Cardinal Virtues, often credited to philosopher Aristocles (more commonly known as Plato). These Cardinal Virtues, aptly named because of the view that all other virtues hinge upon these four, consist of Prudence, Justice, Temperance, and Courage. Aristocles' notion of Prudence may be conceived as the ability to discern the proper course of action, at the appropriate time, in a given situation and with consideration of the potential consequence. Justice may be expressed as the embodiment of fairness, honesty, and impartiality. Temperance is synonymous with self-discipline, restraint, abstention, and moderation. Lastly, Courage may be characterized by resilience, endurance, fortitude, bravery, and the ability to confront fear, uncertainty, and intimidation[4].

In comparison to Aristocles' Four Cardinal Virtues, the Principles of Ma'at encompassed the concepts of Truth, Justice, Harmony, Balance, Order, Propriety, and Reciprocity. The goddess Ma'at was not only the personification of these principles but a standard that citizens were expected to uphold in their daily lives, including in their interactions with family, community, nation, environment, and the Gods. Ma'at was integral to maintaining cosmic harmony and considered essential to the well-being of the state and the individual. It was believed that disturbing the cosmic harmony would have dire consequences, not only for Ancient Khemet, but for all of humanity.

Experience

Italian scientist Leonardo Da Vinci once asserted that "wisdom is the daughter of experience." A catchy maxim, however, is not completely accurate! Experience itself does not impart wisdom. Rather, it is the value of the lessons that we draw from our experiences that lays the foundation for wise thoughts and wise actions. Human cognitive processes enable us to perceive, comprehend, analyze, synthesis, apply, and recall our experiences for future reference. To restate Da Vinci's maxim more accurately, "Wisdom is the daughter of Experience and Cognition."

A common misconception in modern society is that wisdom automatically results from age. While age may be indicative of the number of individual life experiences one may have, it does not necessarily follow that age is indicative of wisdom. Highly intelligent individuals may require fewer experiences to obtain the same level of awareness as someone of average intelligence.

A recent study published in the Journal of Gerontology found that Difficult Life Events (DLEs) promote wisdom as they compel individuals to reevaluate their self-perceptions and how they perceive the world. Difficult life events disrupt an individual's "assumptive world view," which consist of personalized expectations and their orientation toward society (Aldwin, Igarashi and Levenson 2018). Subsequently, dissonance between past and present perceptions is thought to prompt dialectic thinking about self-identity, world views, and life goals. Generally speaking, people who have had to work through difficult life events are the ones who experience transformative growth.

Classifications of Wisdom

So far, our exploration of wisdom has been from a general perspective. Although certain aspects of wisdom are universal and shared across cultures, other characteristics of wisdom overlap between cultures, and some are exclusive to particular cultures. In the following sections we will briefly explore several broad categories of wisdom.

Theoretical, Practical & Intellectual Wisdom

Greek philosopher Aristotle Stagiritis identified three broad categories of wisdom, each reflecting a different approach to knowledge and comprehension. Contemplative or theoretical wisdom (Sophia) is the type of wisdom associated with philosophers. Theoretical wisdom involves the pursuit of ultimate truth and abstract ideas. True philosophers engage in contemplative philosophy, seeking knowledge for the sake of knowledge itself, often delving into metaphysical teachings and philosophical reasoning. Sir. Issac Newton's theory of general relativity is an example of theoretical wisdom. On the other hand, practical wisdom (Phronesis) pertains to the ability to make sound decisions and take appropriate actions in the complex world of human affairs. Practical wisdom enables individuals to navigate the intricacies of social and political life and make informed decisions and ethical choices that are not influenced by personal emotions or sensory misperceptions. Cognitive or intellectual wisdom (Episteme) is scientific or rational understanding. It involves a methodical and systematic approach to knowledge, emphasizing rationality and empirical evidence. Those who possess cognitive wisdom are adept at understanding the nature of things, the principles of causality, and the laws that govern our objective reality.

Conventional vs Emergent Wisdom

American physician, researcher, and inventor Alan R. Khan categorized wisdom into two distinct types: 'conventional wisdom' and "emergent wisdom", the distinction being dependent upon the normative or non-normative environment in which we operate. Conventional wisdom personifies a body of behaviors and norms intended to ameliorate the human experience. Conventional wisdom often results from education and social indoctrination. Thus, it frequently operates beneath the conscious awareness, subtly guiding our thoughts and actions. In scenarios where the environment yields sustainable and stable advantages for individuals, it is conventional wisdom that predominates, serving as a dependable guide.

In circumstances where the milieu experiences a substantial shift, a different modality of wisdom becomes essential. Emergent wisdom is oriented toward innovative transformation of thought and action. During the COVID-19 pandemic, emergent wisdom played an indispensable role in the formulation of novel ideas and behaviors to thwart widespread respiratory illness and death. The desideratum of emergent wisdom normally results from radical changes within the environment in which we are operating (whether that be society, science & technology, education, medicine, or any other domain of the human experience). This necessitates an initial withdrawal from immediate action to develop a more expansive understanding of the diverse elements within these environments. Ultimately, this process culminates in the birth of new, pragmatically viable methodologies.

Personal and General Wisdom

German Psychologist Ursula M. Staudinger proposed that wisdom exist within two primary domains: "personal wisdom" and "general wisdom". The two are differentiated by their reliance on a first-person or third-person ontological perspective. Personal wisdom is a person's insight into his or her personal affairs; that is "the wisdom that a person shows when dealing with uncertain events and problems in their own life." In contrast, general wisdom pertains to the wisdom exhibited in addressing the broader, often communal issues that affect others.

Staudinger's bifurcation of wisdom into "personal" and "general" domains underscores a phenomenon known as 'The Solomon Paradox', named after the biblical King Solomon. This paradox highlights a common human condition where individuals often exhibit greater wisdom in matters concerning others (general wisdom) than in their own personal affairs. It echoes the sentiment of a Chinese proverb, which states, "Spectators see the chess game better than the players." This implies that while some may excel in advising others, they might not necessarily possess the same acumen in their own affairs.

Domain Generality and Depth of Wisdom

American psychologist and psychometrician Dr. Robert J. Sternberg sorts wisdom into four distinct categories. Deep Domain General Wisdom describes individuals capable of comprehensive exploration of complex matters, offering profound insights across various domains. Surface-Level Domain-General Wisdom is reminiscent of wisdom passed to the youth from older generations. This domain involves individuals who can provide moderately insightful advice across a spectrum of domains. Deep Domain-Specific Wisdom centers on profound contemplation of intricate matters within a single domain of inquiry. Surface-Level Domain-Specific Wisdom represents a more superficial level of wisdom. This domain features individuals with moderately insightful knowledge, confined to specific domain of inquiry. An individual will exist as a combination of these domains at almost every moment in their existence.

Humane and Natural Wisdom

The concept of Natural wisdom was first proposed as a counterpart to moral wisdom by Chinese Professor, Dr. Wang Fengyan, at the School of Psychology of Nanjing Normal University. The term "moral wisdom" is attributed to Confucian philosopher Mencius (Master Meg), who suggested that moral wisdom and practical knowledge are the result of long suffering. Natural wisdom encompasses a comprehensive psychological quality that integrates virtue and intelligence, of which moral wisdom is a part. Like its counterpart, natural wisdom is acquired through experience and practice but is grounded in an individual's intelligence and knowledge of the natural world around them.

Humane wisdom embodies a comprehensive psychological attribute that integrates virtue and intelligence, and the broader ethical concern for the welfare of humanity. It emphasizes the application of knowledge and experience in ways that promote the well-being of others and address societal challenges with empathy, moral integrity, and a deep understanding of human nature and social dynamics. Humane wisdom is also acquired through experience and practice but is rooted in an individual's intelligence and knowledge of human society.

Wisdom Pedagogy

Western civilization is now beginning to realize the importance of wisdom and the necessity of developing a pedagogical approach to wisdom in education. Contemporary wisdom pedagogies are altogether inadequate as they fail to develop four key cognitive functions necessary for wise decision-making which are casual analysis, prospection, social cognition, and metacognition (Bracher 2021). These functions are integral to systems thinking, or what our African ancestors referred to as the Cosmic Harmony and are essential for solving global issues.

Casual analysis involves understanding and interpreting the complex network of causes behind problems or situations. It entails identifying and mapping out the numerous factors that contribute to an issue, including direct, indirect, and root causes. This function is essential for accurately diagnosing problems and understanding their complexity. As famously stated by American inventor, engineer, and businessperson Charles Franklin Kettering, "a problem well stated is a problem half solved."

Prospection refers to the ability to look forward and anticipate potential future scenarios. It involves strategic planning and the ability to foresee the consequences of various actions or interventions. Prospection is critical for making decisions that are not only effective in the short term but also sustainable.

Social cognition is about understanding the social dynamics and psychological factors that influence human behavior. It involves the ability to empathize, understand others' perspectives, and consider how people's thoughts, feelings, and social contexts affect their actions and decisions. Social cognition is key to addressing issues that involve human interaction and social systems.

Metacognition is the ability to reflect on and understand one's own thought processes. Metacognition involves self-awareness about how one thinks, learns, and solves problems. It enables individuals to assess their own biases, strengths, and weaknesses in thinking and decision-making. This function is important for continuous learning and improvement in critical thinking.

Together, these cognitive functions form the core of systems thinking and are crucial for addressing complex global challenges in a wise and effective manner. We must emphasize the importance of incorporating these skills into educational pedagogies to foster a generation capable of tackling critical global issues. Implementing a pedagogical approach across disciplines would involve educating students on the nature and harmony of systems and engaging students in developing these key cognitive functions.

Right Wisdom

If wisdom is the quality of having experience, knowledge, and good judgement, Right Wisdom then may be defined as the ability to exercise good judgement in the application of knowledge, intelligence, experience, creativity, and reason in achieving a morally acceptable outcome where the long-term interest of all stakeholders is considered. Our ancient Nubian ancestors pedagogically approached wisdom through the stories of gods, goddesses, and proverbs. To cultivate the necessary wisdom for addressing humanity's modern problems, educational institutions must incorporate a pedagogical approach to cultivating wisdom in our youth.

Right Wisdom, as it relates to Sound Right Reason, emphasizes the critical integration of knowledge, intelligence, experience, creativity, and reason to make morally sound decisions benefiting all stakeholders in the long term. This concept acknowledges the multifaceted nature of wisdom, distinguishing it from mere knowledge and highlighting its reliance on a deep understanding of context and consequences. Sound Right Reason requires that we consider cognitive functions such as causal analysis, prospection, social cognition, and metacognition, essential for developing wisdom. Further, prospection necessitates incorporating these elements into educational practices to effectively address complex global challenges issues.

[1] For more information on hidden African contributions modern civilization please refer to Stolen Legacy by George G.M. James, Ph.D. [2] The wealth of Africa was not its gold, as mistaken believed by many people. The wealth of Africa has always been its knowledge and its people. Remember that many of our modern necessities and luxuries are built on the foundation of numerous African contributions to civilization. This includes, mathematics, algebra, trigonometry, astronomy, medicine, written language, spoken language and more. [3] Inevitably, all humans must experience death. Whether or not this can be viewed as a function that we perform excellently is left to individual perspective. Nevertheless, it is a function that all humans must perform and as such it is essential to and a virtue of being human. At least according to the early Greek philosopher's definition of Virtue. [4] The Greek word for Courage (ANDREIA) is more closely aligned with the English words for manliness or masculinity.

5

What is Right Overstanding?

Many may disagree with the use of the term 'overstand' in serious discourse and dismiss it as slang or Ebonics. This perspective not only diminishes African American culture and contributions to the broader American society, but it also disregards the phenomenon of semantic shift. Semantic shift or semantic change is a linguistic process wherein the connotations and usage of a word evolves, often diverging significantly from its original meaning. This process is common in language development. There are numerous instances within American English wherein semantic shift has fundamentally altered word meanings. For instance, the term 'awful,' which initially signified "full of awe" or impressive, has undergone such a semantic transition. Modern definitions of word 'awful' encompass and are generally orientated toward meaning "extremely bad or unpleasant; terrible." Similarly, 'terrific,' once denoting "inspiring terror," has evolved to describe something "extraordinary or exceptionally good."

The term 'overstand' is not a novel word originating within Pan-African nationalist pro-black communities. The term 'overstand' has its roots in the Old English word oferstandan ("to stand over"), which is equivalent to over + stand. It is cognate with the Dutch word overstaan ("to stand over"), and the German word Überstehen ("to stand through, survive"). Historically, its connotation encompassed the ability to endure or withstand challenges, persist beyond necessity, or to adhere rigorously to demands or conditions. The origin of its contemporary usage, suggesting a level of comprehension beyond a basic understanding, is the topic of debate. This further underscore the intriguing aspect of linguistic evolution and the dynamic nature of language, as specially as it relates to the influence of evolving subcultures.

Varying levels of comprehension

Collectively, the terms understand, overstand, and innerstand denote varying levels of comprehension. Understanding is defined as the act of comprehending the meaning, nature or importance of a thing, or awareness of something. "Overstand" is a term that is used, particularly in Pan-African cultures, to conveys the idea of achieving a higher level of comprehension or mastery that surpasses a basic understanding. It reflects a state of elevated awareness, often connected to transformative experiences. "Innerstanding" is a term that is used, particularly in spiritual or metaphysical contexts, to denote a deeper level of comprehension that goes beyond intellectual understanding and involves a profound sense of inner awareness, internalization, or insight.

Tripartite approach to comprehension

The notion of a tripartite hierarchical framework for comprehension is well-established in the world of psychology and academia. In 1982, Lane Roy Gauthier embarked on an extensive research endeavor, culminating in the submission and subsequent publication of his doctoral dissertation and theses. The central focus of Gauthier's work was to elucidate the inherent disparity among the three primary levels of comprehension: literal, inferential, and critical (evaluative), as they pertain to cognitive demand (Gauthier, Lane Roy; Lousiana State University and Agricultural & Mechanical College 1982).

Understanding (Literal Comprehension)

Comprehension varies among individuals based on their education, experiences, and the complexity of the subject matter in consideration. Literal comprehension or 'understanding' denotes a basic awareness and is manifested through the procurement of information related to specific questions normally prefaced by "what, where, when, who," and so forth. This level of comprehension includes identifying main ideas, recalling supporting details, and understanding the order of events. Literal comprehension is fundamental, allowing recognition of clear, surface-level details in written or spoken content. It is essential as a foundation for more advanced comprehension, requiring one to grasp the explicit meaning of sentences and words without deeper analysis. Likewise, Literal Comprehension is required to recall trivial details and arrange pivotal occurrences in chronological order. It transpires at a rudimentary level, wherein the observer recognizes observable and audible content. The details of which are readily identifiable. Literal comprehension represents the most elementary stratum of comprehension and constitutes the foundation upon which more sophisticated levels of comprehension are developed.

Overstanding (Inference Comprehension)

Inferential comprehension (overstanding) encompasses the ability to draw logical conclusions from information and data presented or recalled from a text, oration, narratives, or experience. Cognitively, inference (overstanding) requires the individual to traverse beyond explicit statements, through a heightened level of engagement that goes beyond mere observation, discerning meaning that is implied rather than explicitly stated. At this level of comprehension, individuals seek to address questions that consider the rationale or processes behind phenomena, typically introduced with "Why" and "How."

Human inference capabilities are deeply rooted in our evolutionary development. This uncanny ability has played a pivotal role in shaping our cognitive processes. It is well beyond the purview of this particular chapter to delve into a comprehensive elucidation of human inference, as it is nonessential in accentuating the importance of this cognitive process in the science and system of Nuwaubu. Nevertheless, we will briefly discuss certain intricacies inherent in these abilities, distinctive characteristics, and their indispensable role in shaping our decision-making processes. We will also revisit human inference, as it relates to the cognitive processes in a later chapter.

The human Inferential processes can be broadly categorized into conscious, semiconscious, and unconscious modalities. Conscious inferences are discernible by their adaptability, flexibility, and constrained by the limitations of working memory. Conversely, unconscious inferences are swift, outside of our immediate awareness, and lack the malleability of their conscious counterparts. Semiconscious inferences occur during a state of imperfect awareness. For example, when daydreaming the mind wanders and attention becomes divided between internal and external information, this is known as the decoupling of attention. Daydreaming produces a state of semiconscious inferences, wherein attention is decoupled from awareness, and focused inward towards one's thoughts and feelings. Although aware, individuals struggle to effectively integrate information from the external environment.

At the core of human cognition reside two fundamental categories of inference: deductive and inductive. Deductive inferences, aimed at preserving truth and rendering implicit knowledge explicit, are instrumental in maintaining the consistency of belief systems and worldviews. Nevertheless, deductive inferences are limited to the capacity of the working memory and contingent on the nuances of content and context. As previously discussed, comprehension varies among individuals based on their education, experience, and the complexity of the subject in consideration. An individual's level of familiarity with the subject matter bares a significant impact on the evaluation of deductive arguments, with logically structured arguments proving more intelligible. Arguments laden with inconsistencies or false and misleading premises tend to present greater cognitive challenges.

Inductive reasoning encompasses inferences that transform initial information based on implicit assumptions about the structure of the world and how it operates. It relies extensively on representativeness heuristic, thus introducing an element of risk into the inference process. Representativeness heuristic entails estimating the probability of an object, event, or relation in the real world based on how typical it seems compared to one's own concepts and individual experiences. These implicit assumptions are the mechanisms that govern the transformation of information. Risk arises from the possibility that the presuppositions underlying the inference may prove false in a given situation, leading to a false belief. This trade-off means that while initial information's truth does not guarantee the conclusion's truth, good inductive inferences generate highly probable conclusions based on true (right) initial information.

Inferential comprehension, encompassing both deductive and inductive reasoning, is crucial for drawing logical conclusions and understanding complex phenomena. However, it is not without its limitations. Deductive reasoning can lead to flawed conclusions if based on incorrect premises, and inductive reasoning can be biased by subjective experiences and assumptions. These limitations underscore the need for critical evaluation and validation of premises and observations to ensure sound reasoning and accurate inferences, maintaining the integrity of the decision-making process in the system of Nuwaubu.

Innerstanding (Evaluative Comprehension)

The third strata of comprehension, evaluative comprehension (Innerstanding), demands an even deeper engagement with the subject matter.

This level of advanced comprehension requires the observer to transcend mere content analysis. It involves a critical assessment and interpretation of various aspects of the subject matter, such as the underlying themes, the author's intent, opinion, and the stylistic nuances of the presentation. Evaluative comprehension is pivotal in forming holistic view of the subject matter, as it entails not just processing the content at face value, but also critically examining and appraising its broader implications and underpinnings, internalization, and formulation of an authentic point of view.

My hope is that our exploration into the concept of Right Overstanding will impress upon the audience an enlightened view of the intricate and multifaceted nature of comprehension. Through knowledge of the origins and evolution of the term "overstand," we awaken a deeper appreciation for the richness and transformative power of language in our lives. The tripartite approach to comprehension serves as a framework for recognizing and nurturing our cognitive abilities. By honing our literal (understanding), inferential (overstanding), and evaluative (innerstanding) comprehension capabilities, we equip ourselves to navigate the intricacies of knowledge acquisition and cultivate a more profound awareness and engagement with the world.

The notion of Right Overstanding illuminates the significance of varying levels of comprehension within the linguistic and cultural contexts of communities of color. It challenges dismissive views of terms like "overstand," underscoring its relevance in conveying deeper comprehension beyond basic understanding. This exploration not only celebrates linguistic evolution but also emphasizes the cognitive depth required for meaningful engagement with ideas and narratives. By embracing terms like over- and innerstand, individuals enhance their ability to critically analyze and interpret information, fostering a more nuanced understanding of language's transformative power in shaping perceptions and worldviews.

6

What is Sound Right Reason?

At its core Nuwaubu is the Science of Sound Right Reason! Reason, as it applies here, is the capacity for rational thought. The human capacity to reason is limited to the here and now, and our ability to create is limited to the culmination of our life experiences. If we were to look at technology over the past century you would begin to notice that all technological advancements are based on and consist of existing technologies. These technologies are either enhanced, recalibrated, or repurposed creating new use cases. I have yet to meet a human with the ability to contemplate a truly foreign and novel idea. One in which neither the object nor any of its component parts have never been contemplated. Nevertheless, it is our ability to reason that separates humanity from the rest of our planetary cohabitants. Inherent to human nature is the inclination to engage in intuitive thinking, where initial information is subject to rational analysis, leading to a deeper understanding. This process empowers us to evaluate alternative courses of action and select the one that best serves our interests. However, this natural inclination does not render the human species perfectly rational. Over the course of this next chapter, we will briefly discuss humanity's unique ability to reason and the constraints that limit our ability to achieve perfect rationality.

The Human Ability to Reason

Human reasoning is one of the most distinctive and profound capabilities of mankind, and while remarkable it is not without its limitations.

Despite our ability to analyze information, solve problems, and make decisions our reasoning processes are often flawed and susceptible to various biases and errors. We will briefly explore the inherent limitations of human reasoning, examining the cognitive biases, emotional influences, and logical fallacies that can hinder our ability to think clearly and make sound judgments. We will delve into the ways in which our reasoning can be compromised, from the influence of confirmation bias to the impact of cognitive dissonance. By understanding these limitations, we can become more aware of the potential pitfalls in our thinking and develop strategies to mitigate their effects. Through this exploration, we aim to shed light on the challenges we face in achieving truly rational thought and to highlight the importance of critical thinking and self-awareness in overcoming these obstacles. We will briefly discuss seven broad, non-exhaustive categories of reasoning [1]:

Deductive Reasoning

Deductive reasoning employs formal logic and empirical observations to validate a theory or hypothesis. In this process, you begin with a problem statement, formulate a viable hypothesis, gather, and measure relevant data, assess and analyze that data, and subsequently confirm or reject your hypothesis. Two prevalent criteria are used to evaluate arguments when applying deductive reasoning. Validity pertains to the logical connection between the premises and the conclusion. An argument is considered valid when the premise provides logical support and relevance to the conclusion. However, in deductive reasoning, the truth of the premises does not guarantee a true solution. Soundness, on the other hand, denotes a condition in which an argument is both valid and possesses true premises.

Inductive Reasoning

Inductive reasoning involves using established theories and assumptions to validate observations and draw general conclusions. However, conclusions derived from inductive reasoning are inherently uncertain. The Problem of Induction centers around the fact that future events are not necessarily predicated upon past occurrences. For instance, let us consider flipping a standard U.S. quarter forty-nine times, with each toss resulting in tails. Despite this sequence, there still remains a 50% chance that the coin will land on heads in the next flip. Following inductive reasoning one might argue that there is a 100% chance the coin will land on tails based on its consistent history of the past forty-nine flips.

Analogical Reasoning

Analogical reasoning is a cognitive process that identifies similarities between two or more entities and utilizes these similarities to uncover additional commonalities. Analogical reasoning is rooted in the human brain's innate inclination to recognize patterns and establish associations. As these patterns become more apparent, the mind draws parallels between specific elements, giving rise to analogical reasoning. The capacity to perceive and apply relational similarities between two scenarios or events is a fundamental aspect of human cognition. This capacity represents a pivotal cognitive mechanism that distinguishes human cognition from that of other intelligent species. Although analogical reasoning offers significant potential, it is important to acknowledge its limitations and potential drawbacks. Over-reliance on analogies can lead to oversimplification, confirmation bias, and erroneous conclusions. To mitigate these risks, it is imperative that we complement analogical reasoning with other critical thinking and analytical approaches. This balanced approach acts as a cognitive safety net, safeguarding against the pitfalls of flawed reasoning.

Abductive Reasoning

Abductive Reasoning is a mode of reasoning that employs the use of one or more observations to arrive at a rational conclusion. Abductive Reasoning allows for the formulation of well-informed conjectures to arrive at the simplest conclusions. Abductive Reasoning is an invaluable tool in troubleshooting and decision making, especially where uncertainty is involved. Abductive Reasoning is especially useful in clarifying an observation or phenomenon for which the observer has little or no prior knowledge. Outcomes derived from Abductive Reasoning carry a degree of uncertainty and warrant further validation because it involves generating hypotheses based on limited observations, and these hypotheses are inherently uncertain and speculative. Unlike deductive reasoning, which looks to validate a theory or hypothesis, abductive reasoning seeks the most likely or plausible explanation.

Casualty

Casualty, also referred to as Cause-and-effect reasoning, is a form of reasoning that illustrates the relationship between two occurrences. It serves the purpose of explaining the possible consequences of specific actions or the underlying factors behind events occurring under certain conditions. Cause-and-effect reasoning is a fundamental aspect of everyday decision-making, where individuals rely on personal experience and a desire for improvement. It is vital to watch for false cause fallacies, which may occur where one incorrectly assumes a causal connection between two unrelated things or events. Additionally, there exist instances where multiple causes contribute to a single effect or where a single cause leads to a variety of outcomes.

Critical Thinking

Critical thinking is a mode of reasoning that involves thorough and methodical examination of a specific subject with the objective of arriving at a comprehensive solution. This cognitive approach is advantageous in domains such as computing, engineering, social sciences, and logic. Critical thinking plays a pivotal role in problem-solving intricate technical issues. Nevertheless, there are challenges associated with critical thinking, which often center around individual abilities and factors such as over-reliance on emotions, subjective judgments, egocentric or biased thinking, subconscious biases or selective perception, closed-mindedness, inadequate communication skills or indifference, and a deficiency in personal integrity, among other factors.

Decompositional Reasoning

Decompositional reasoning involves the process of reducing entities into their constituent parts to gain a deeper understanding of the function of each individual component and its relationship to the overall system. Through an isolated analysis of component parts, decompositional reasoning empowers an observer to extract valuable holistic insights. This approach is prevalent in fields such as science, engineering, marketing, product development, gaming, and software development. In the context of project management, decompositional reasoning plays a critical role in segmenting projects into manageable components. Each segment is then assigned to an individual who is responsible for its execution and integration into the project. This segmentation ensures the success of individual components and contributes to the success of the overall project. One notable consideration of decompositional reasoning revolves around the concept of synergy. Synergy occurs when the combined effect of individual components working in concert exceeds the sum of their individual contributions.

Limitation in the Human Ability to Reason

Each of the various types of reasoning discussed within this chapter provides a structured approach to engaging with information, verifying assumptions, and reaching an informed conclusion. When aptly applied they contribute to the validity of an argument by providing distinct methodologies to approach and analyze information, offering complementary perspectives and methodologies that collectively strengthen the rigor and reliability of decision making and comprehension across various domains of inquiry. This integration of diverse reasoning methods promotes a holistic and robust framework for navigating complexities and deriving meaningful insights in both personal and intellectual pursuits. However, their effectiveness depends on context, quality of information, and the ability to mitigate their respective flaws. Remaining open to revising hypotheses based on new evidence helps mitigate these limitations and enhances the validity and reliability of decision-making processes.

It is crucial that we have accurate information, wisdom in interpreting it correctly, and a deepened comprehension of the subject matter when choosing a method of reasoning for several reasons. Accurate information forms the foundation of any logical reasoning process. Without accurate data or facts (Right Knowledge), the conclusions drawn may be flawed or misleading. Right Wisdom in interpretation ensures that the information is not only accurate but also relevant and contextualized correctly within the subject matter. Different situations call for different types of reasoning. For instance, deductive reasoning relies on true premises, while inductive reasoning deals with probabilities based on observations. A true overstanding of the subject matter helps in recognizing its biases, assumptions, or oversimplifications that may affect the reasoning process.

Cognitive Dissonance

Reflecting on our previous dialogue on comprehension, we learned that the human mind possesses two distinct modalities of inference. The origins of which are deeply rooted in human evolutionary development. Inductive inference involves the application of accepted truths and suppositions to substantiate observations and draw general conclusions. Deductive inferences are directed toward the preservation of accepted truth, clarification of tacit knowledge, and involves the use of logic and empirical observations to validate or refute a theory or hypothesis. Deductive inferences are instrumental in maintaining the consistency of belief systems and worldviews. We rely on two essential criteria when evaluating arguments. Validity concerns the logical connection between the premises and the eventual conclusion. An argument is considered valid when its premises lend logical support and relevance to the conclusion. However, the veracity of the premises does not necessarily guarantee an accurate resolution. Soundness, on the other hand, is an attribute ascribed to an argument when it is both valid and possess a true premises.

At any given moment, the human mind is engaged in the continuous process of constructing inferences. This inferential mechanism equips humanity with the capacity to navigate and adapt to their environment by transforming information, cultivating new information, discerning, and potentially reconciling inconsistent information. At times we are acutely aware and fully engaged with this cognitive progression. Others transpire within the penumbra of our awareness, occurring at a realm that straddles subconscious and unconscious layers of thought. Psychological discomfort, known as cognitive dissonance, results when our attitude, behavior, and feelings contradict with simultaneously held beliefs, ideas, and values compelling individuals to reconsider these cognitions to resolve the inconsistency causing the mental stress. The concept of cognitive dissonance was first introduced by American psychologist Leon Festinger, PhD in his 1957 book entitled A Theory of Cognitive Dissonance (Festinger 1962).

Theoretical Paradigms of Cognitive Dissonance

Cognitive dissonance, the psychological conflict experienced when one's beliefs are challenged by contradictory evidence or behaviors, is a condition unrestrained by background or belief. For African American people, whose genetic memory encompasses the harrowing passages of the transatlantic slave trade to the continuous strivings for identity and equality in the western hemisphere, cognitive dissonance manifests through a variety of complex experiences. We will briefly examine several theoretical paradigms of cognitive dissonance prevalent among Americans in general and African American's specifically. Each paradigm offers a unique lens through which we can analyze the historical and contemporary struggles of the African American people. By synapsing these paradigms, I hope to highlight obscure psychological forces that have shaped and continue to influence the journey of African American people as we strive to reconcile the reality of our tumultuous past with a future deserving of our people.

Induced Compliance

Induced compliance specifically refers to scenarios in which individuals behave in ways that contradict their deeply held personal beliefs, convictions, or values because of external pressures or duress. Such pressures can emanate from our peers, family members, employers, or even society at large. The mechanisms through which forced compliance is achieved are diverse and complex, ranging from overt forms of aggression like physical violence and explicit threats to more subtle and insidious tactics including coercion, manipulation, and various forms of psychological abuse. Psychological abuse, for example, can take the shape of bullying or ostracism, each designed to exploit vulnerabilities and exert control, thereby creating an environment wherein the individual feels compelled to act against their better judgment or personal ethical standards.

Belief Disconfirmation Paradigm

The Belief Disconfirmation paradigm centers around the psychological conflict that arises when we, as often a result of our inherent human inference capabilities, prematurely commit to certain beliefs, ideals, or values without exploring all necessary and relevant information. Specifically, this paradox explores the cognitive dissonance experienced when we encounter new contradictory information, challenging our premature commitments beliefs, ideas, or values. The Belief Disconfirmation paradigm underscores the natural human tendency to develop strong attachments to our viewpoints and the discomfort we face when confronted with evidence that directly opposes our preconceived notions. This dissonance not only highlights the fluidity of our belief systems but also prompts a psychological and sometimes behavioral response as we strive to reconcile our established beliefs with new, conflicting information. The process is indicative of the dynamic nature of human cognition, illustrating how our understanding and beliefs are continually shaped by the interplay between existing convictions and added information.

Confirmation Bias Paradigm

The confirmation bias paradigm is the tendency for people to seek, interpret, and remember information that supports their existing beliefs while giving less attention to contradictory evidence. These biases influence decision-making, perception, and information processing. One key aspect is the selective search for evidence, where individuals seek information that supports their beliefs, such as someone with strong political views only reading news that agrees with their perspective. Another aspect is the interpretation of ambiguous evidence in a way that supports their pre-existing ideas. Memory and recall are also affected, as people tend to remember supportive information and forget contradictory information. After a debate, for instance, someone might recall points that matched their opinion and ignore those that did not. Lastly, confirmation bias can lead to overconfidence, as people become too sure of their beliefs by undervaluing contradictory evidence. Understanding this paradigm is crucial, as it highlights how a common bias can impact judgment and decision-making. By recognizing and addressing confirmation bias, individuals and organizations can make more accurate judgments and better decisions.

Free Choice Paradigm

The Free Choice paradigm illuminates the psychological turmoil we undergo when confronted with the necessity to make a choice between two or more alternatives. This phenomenon occurs in situations where the options before us carry similar levels of attractiveness or aversiveness, compelling us to make a decision that inevitably leads to the exclusion of one or more equally compelling choices (This is the literal definition of a dilemma). The act of making such a choice induces a state of psychological dissonance, primarily because selecting one option over another can lead to regret or second-guessing, particularly given the closely aligned desirability of the alternatives. The resulting cognitive dissonance stems from the internal conflict between the value we see in the chosen alternative and the value we must forsake in the options not chosen, highlighting the intricate psychological dynamics at play when we exercise our freedom to choose, especially under conditions of close competition between alternatives.

Forbidden Behavior Paradigm

The forbidden behavior paradigm describes scenarios where individuals are instructed to refrain from a particular behavior, which can inadvertently heighten their desire to indulge said behavior. The allure of the action intensifies due to its prohibition. Cognitive dissonance is introduced when the individual experiences internal conflict between their desire to indulge the forbidden behavior and the directive to abstain.

Likewise, succumbing to temptation causes cognitive dissonance because of the misalignment between their conduct and the established directive. To alleviate psychological discomfort, the individual may rationalize their disobedience, convincing themselves that the directive is excessively restrictive or trivializing the gravity of the forbidden act.

The Effects of Cognitive Dissonance on Decision Making

Cognitive dissonance impacts decision-making by creating psychological discomfort when an individual holds conflicting beliefs, attitudes, or behaviors. This discomfort can lead to rationalization of choices, where individuals justify their decisions by emphasizing positives and downplaying negatives. For instance, after buying an expensive car, a person might highlight its features and status while minimizing concerns about the cost. Additionally, cognitive dissonance can cause people to avoid conflicting information, leading to poor decision-making. For example, someone who invests in a particular stock may ignore negative reports about the company, resulting in a skewed view and potentially flawed decisions.

Furthermore, cognitive dissonance can lead to biased information processing, where individuals favor data that supports their beliefs and disregard or misinterpret contradictory information. This bias can result in incomplete or inaccurate decision-making. The stress and anxiety caused by holding conflicting cognitions can impair judgment, leading to hasty or irrational choices. In business, this often manifests as an escalation of commitment, where managers continue to invest in failing projects to avoid admitting a mistake. Cognitive dissonance can also impact integrity and ethics, causing individuals to justify unethical behavior to align with their actions. To resolve dissonance, individuals might change their beliefs or attitudes to match their decisions, such as aligning with a political candidate's platform post-vote. Understanding these effects helps individuals and organizations recognize and mitigate biases, leading to more balanced and rational decision-making.

Cognitive Dissonance Among African American People

Cognitive dissonance among African Americans is deeply influenced by the concept of dual consciousness. Introduced by W.E.B. Du Bois, dual consciousness creates an internal conflict between one's self-perception and the perception imposed by society. This conflict can significantly impact an individual's identity, leading to a fragmented sense of self. African Americans often find themselves reconciling their personal identity with societal stereotypes and expectations. The struggle to integrate individual experiences and cultural heritage with societal norms can make it difficult to develop a cohesive identity. For instance, they may feel torn between their cultural heritage and the need to conform to mainstream American culture, resulting in a fragmented identity.

This duality can also lead to feelings of alienation and marginalization. The pressure to fit into both Black and non-Black communities can result in feelings of alienation from both groups, leading to social isolation and a diminished sense of belonging. Moreover, the experience of being marginalized in a society that often devalues or misunderstands one's racial or cultural identity exacerbates feelings of exclusion and erodes self-esteem. The constant negotiation between two conflicting identities can cause significant psychological stress, leading to cognitive dissonance. Prolonged exposure can result in an identity crisis, affecting mental health and overall well-being. Despite these challenges, navigating and reconciling dual identities can foster empowerment and resilience, enabling individuals to celebrate their heritage while engaging with broader societal contexts and advocating for social change and justice.

Reconciling Cognitive Dissonance

Perfectly Rational

A perfectly rational human being would resolve cognitive dissonance through intentional and logical steps aimed at aligning their beliefs, attitudes, and behaviors with relevant information. This would start with identifying the source of dissonance through a process of self-reflection, examining specific beliefs, attitudes, or behaviors that are in conflict. Objective analysis of the conflicting elements would follow, ensuring a clear grasp of the nature and extent of the conflict. Next, a perfectly rational human being would gather comprehensive information, researching and evaluating evidence from credible sources and considering multiple perspectives to ensure their conclusions are based on sound evidence.

A perfectly rational human being would then consider alternative perspectives, remaining open to added information and viewpoints, even if these viewpoints contradict their current beliefs. Engaging with others to obtain feedback can provide additional insights and help identify blind spots in our reasoning. A perfectly rational human being would then evaluate the consequences of maintaining conflicting beliefs versus resolving the dissonance, considering the long-term impact of their decisions. If the evidence supports a particular viewpoint, a perfectly rational human being would adjust their beliefs to align with the evidence or modify their behavior to be consistent with rationally evaluated beliefs. Implementing changes gradually, monitoring progress, and maintaining ethical standards throughout the process ensures a smooth transition and builds trust, achieving a harmonious alignment between beliefs and actions, minimizing psychological discomfort, and enhancing decision-making.

Perfectly Imperfect

Resolving cognitive dissonance is a complex process, especially since human beings are not perfectly rational. Our decisions and beliefs are heavily influenced by emotions, biases, and our subjective experiences. Thus, making it increasingly challenging to consistently align our actions with our beliefs. Despite our best intentions, we often rationalize conflicting behaviors or adjust our beliefs to reduce psychological discomfort. This inherent irrationality requires a thoughtful and systematic approach to address cognitive dissonance.

The subjective functions of the objective mind play a crucial role in resolving cognitive dissonance. While the objective mind seeks logical consistency, our subjective experiences influence how we perceive and interpret information. This duality means that even when presented with unmistakable evidence, our personal biases and emotions can shape our understanding and response. Recognizing this interplay between objectivity and subjectivity is essential for addressing cognitive dissonance, as it helps us identify the underlying factors that contribute to conflicting beliefs and behaviors.

For African American people, reconciling cognitive dissonance is vital to achieving a state of Sound Right Reason. This concept emphasizes the importance of aligning one's beliefs, actions, and values to foster mental clarity and integrity. Given the historical and societal challenges faced by black people, addressing cognitive dissonance can lead to a stronger, more cohesive self-identity and community. Systematically examining and resolving internal conflicts and building on a foundation of right knowledge, right wisdom, and right overstanding are essential for personal growth and community empowerment. By adopting a systematic approach to addressing cognitive dissonance, individuals can achieve greater mental clarity, integrity, and alignment between their beliefs and behaviors, leading to improved decision-making and personal well-being.

[1] This list is not intended to be mutually exclusive or collectively exhaustive.

7

The Philosophical Science of Nuwaubu

Everything that we have explored up until this point has been laying a foundation for approaching Nuwaubu as the philosophical Science of Sound Right Reasoning. In this context, philosophical science encompasses the observation, identification, description, experimental investigation, and theoretical explanation of the fundamental nature of knowledge, reality, and existence. We have emphasized the importance of accurate and complete information (Right Knowledge) as the bedrock upon which objective opinions are formed. We have explored the concept of Wisdom, differentiated it from knowledge, and accentuated the importance of virtue (Ma'at) in wise thinking and wise actions. We have contemplated the concept of Overstanding in the context of a tripartite approach to comprehension. Lastly, we have deepened our understanding of diverse forms of reasoning, recognizing their individual strengths, limitations, and the critical importance of maintaining balanced approaches in the realm of critical thinking.

In this chapter, we shall conjoin the notions of Right Knowledge, Right Wisdom, and Right Overstanding into a structured approach to Sound Right Reasoning. Beginning with a quick glance into the Khemetic roots of philosophy and how the early Greek philosophers unknowingly commandeered it. Furthermore, we shall endeavor to explicitly establish the necessity of Nuwaubu as a scientific approach to living and advocate for its adoption within African American Communities. Through this journey into the Philosophy of Nuwaubu, we shall endeavor to uncover the timeless wisdom embedded within its principles and illuminate its transformative potential in shaping our understanding of self, existence, and the cosmos at large.

The Khemetic Origins of Philosophy

The English word Philosophy results from the conjunction of the Greek word Philo (φίλος) which is often translated as love but is better translated as "friend" or "companion" and a Greek word of unknown origin, Sophia (σοφία) which is an abstract noun of Sophós (σοφός), and incorrectly presumed to imply "clever, skillful, intelligent or wise". However, as pointed out by Dutch linguist Robert S.P. Beekes, the etymology of the Greek words Sophia (σοφία) and Sophós (σοφός) are impossible to trace and are likely stratum[1] (Beekes, Ph.D. and van Beek, Ph.D. 2016). Sophia's unknown etymological origin is rooted in the fact that prior to its introduction by Socrates, there existed no Greek concept of wisdom separate and apart from knowledge.

Historians will suggest to us that ancient Greeks considered wisdom to be an important virtue, personified as the goddesses Metis. Metis, an Oceanid, was the first wife of Zeus who, according to Hesiod's Theogony, had been devoured by the 'King of the Olympians' while pregnant with their first-born Athena (White 1914). If you will recall from our previous discourse on Right Wisdom, the concept of virtue (ARETE) for ancient Greeks is aligned with the notion of function (ERGON), it disregards morality and concern itself with only the excellent performance of any function.

Hesiod's Theogony, the first known Greek cosmogony, composed between 730-700 BCE, is the earliest and most detailed account of Metis. Hesiod's Theogony is an epic poem that describes the origins and genealogies of the Greek gods. According to this epic, the initial state of the cosmos (universe) was chaos, a dark indefinite void considered a driving primordial condition from which everything else appears. From Chaos sprang the first deathless gods, namely Gaia (Earth), Tartarus (Underworld), Eros (Desire), Erebus (Darkness), and Nyx (Night). Gaia brought forth her equal and husband Uranus (Sky). Metis was the daughter of Oceanus, the first-born son Uranus and Gaia, and his sister Tethys. By the fifth century BC, Metis had been attributed the titles of good counsel, prudence, deep thought, and higher wisdom. Suggesting that "Metis" implies "craft", "skill", and "wisdom." However, its original connotation implied "magical cunning" and trickery, as displayed in her liberation of the Titans and her involvement in the battles of Zeus.

Historians will try to foist upon us that Greek mythology dates back to the Bronze Age, which began around 3200 BCE suggesting that the mythology of ancient Greece was passed down orally before being document in written form during the Archaic (c. 800-480 BCE) and Classical periods (c, 480-323 BCE) periods. Admittingly, historians will acknowledge the influence of Minoan, Mycenaean, and other so-called 'Mediterranean' civilizations while negating the influence of vastly superior Nile Valley and other Nubian Civilization who, by the Bronze Age, had already begun documenting in written form their laws, cosmologies, cosmogonies, and various "ologies" (Amen 2019).

If you have ever studied Egyptian theology, Greek theology should sound vaguely familiar. The ancient Greek notion of deity (gods and goddesses) is but an impression of African Theology. Like much of the world, Greece was heavily influenced, whether directly or indirectly, by the ancient African civilizations who western scholars have tried to bury beneath the pages of history. Many of the foundational concepts of Western philosophy, particularly those attributed to the ancient Greeks, were actually derived from African intellectual traditions. Early Greek philosophers such as Pythagoras, Socrates, and Plato were influenced by, and in the case of Pythagoras and Socrates were initiates of, the "Mysteries." Sadly, African contributions to philosophy, mathematics, chemistry, medicine, astronomy, language, geography, civics, music, and art have been systematically destroyed or ignored by mainstream historical narratives, perpetuating a Eurocentric view of intellectual history. Nevertheless, African civilizations, particularly those of the Nile River Valley, have played a pivotal role in the development of human knowledge and culture.

Just outside the modern city of Cairo, Egypt, stands three great marvels of the ancient world: the tombs of A'aferti Khufu, A'aferti Khafre, and A'aferti Menkaure. These awe-inspiring structures, erected between 2550 and 2490 BCE, have endured unassisted for more than 4,500 years, captivating the fascination of contemporary society. The enigmatic allure of Nile Valley Civilizations, spanning from Khoisan to Ancient Khemet and Nubia, is undeniable. Yet, our knowledge of these remarkable civilizations, which meticulously documented their extraordinary accomplishments across various domains, from architecture to astronomy, remains shrouded in mystery. Looting, hoarding, and the deliberate destruction of records and artifacts have undoubtedly contributed to the large gaps in our understanding of these cultures. Notably, the construction of the Khazan Aswan (Aswan Low) Dam by British engineers in 1902 and the as-Sad al-'Aali (Aswan High) Dam by Egyptian President Gamal Abdel Nasser Hussein in 1976 serves as poignant reminders of the racially motivated destruction of African heritage (Carruthers 2023).

Hieroglyphs, once indecipherable, have only recently become accessible with the discovery of the Rosetta Stone and have led to a broader understanding of Ancient Egypt. The Rosetta Stone was created by remnants of the Egyptian Brotherhood for the specific purpose of translating Egyptian scrolls for Alexander III of Macedonia and Aristotle. These scrolls would later be organized into the 400+ books attributed to, but actually plagiarized by, Aristotle (James 1954). Over the centuries, the interests and biases of historians have significantly influenced the focus of research and reporting. Most ancient "African" cultures and facets within these civilizations have received inadequate attention, altogether ignored, or interpreted through biased lenses.

The Philosophical Science of Nuwaubu

Nuwaubu, as a Philosophical Science, is a practical and systematic approach to studying the nature, causes, or principles of reality, knowledge, or values based on Sound Right Reason. It is characteristic of a well-balanced thought process and grounded in truth. Nuwaubu is not static nor dogmatic, but open to the dynamic and evolving nature of information and adaptable to the realities of life and the complexities of the modern world.

The attainment of Sound Right Reason is predicated on Right Knowledge, Right Wisdom, and Right Overstanding. The first step in the system of Nuwaubu is ensuring that we have Right Knowledge. Right Knowledge being defined as a state of knowledge obtained through in-depth study of accurate and complete scientific facts and information. Right knowledge is exact, objective, and always based on facts. The same is true irrespective of our inability to reconcile such facts with our current system of belief and personal views.

We have established that knowledge alone is insufficient in producing the sagacious mode of thinking required for navigating the complexities of modern life. Therefore, we must exercise Right Wisdom in all consequential decisions. Distinct from knowledge, Right Wisdom is the ability to exercise good judgement in the application of knowledge, intelligence, experience, creativity, and reason in achieving a morally acceptable outcome. Most modern definitions of wisdom emphasize a concern for the welfare of humanity as prerequisite wise for decisions and wise actions. Consequently, Right Wisdom requires an outcome in which the long-term interest of all stakeholders is considered.

Efficacious use of Nuwaubu requires a level of engagement and comprehension beyond that of a basic understanding. Inference Comprehension (Overstanding) encompasses the ability to draw logical conclusions from information and data presented or recalled from a text, oration, narrative, or experience. Right Overstanding requires that we move beyond mere observation, discerning implied meaning to address questions that consider the rationale or processes behind phenomena.

Nuwaubu transcends linearity; there is no fixed sequence that one must follow in attaining a state of Sound Right Reason. Rather, it necessitates a comprehensive and integrative examination of the prerequisite conditions. In life, we will often find that problems do not present themselves in conveniently bundled packages with all pertinent information and instructions for the optimal approach in addressing them. Nevertheless, we can take comfort in knowing that our conjectures are well-informed and grounded in a foundation of educated reasoning.

The Endangered Black Male

My brothers, it is imperative that I devote a portion of this book to speaking directly to you, in an attempt to impress upon you the gravity of our abysmal situation here in America. At this very moment there is cruel and nefarious deception being perpetrated against us. Black men here in America face a range of challenges, from systemic inequalities to the challenges of social dynamics, which are unparalleled by any other demographic group within this country. We experience higher rates of unemployment and underemployment compared to other demographics, and twice that of white men and white women. We often encounter barriers to career advancement, wage gaps, and limited access to economic opportunities and public assistance. There are disparities in educational attainment from early childhood through higher education. As the progenitors of human civilization, we deserve better than this harrowing situation that we are perpetuating and perpetrating against our-selves.

African American men are seriously falling far behind in the area of educational attainment. As a demographic group we tend to have lower high school graduation rates, lower college enrollment rates, and significantly lower college and advance degree completion rates. According to The Brookings Institution[2], young black males have the lowest high school graduation rate of any demographic, including young black females, who in 2021, graduated at a rate of 85% compared to 76% for black males.

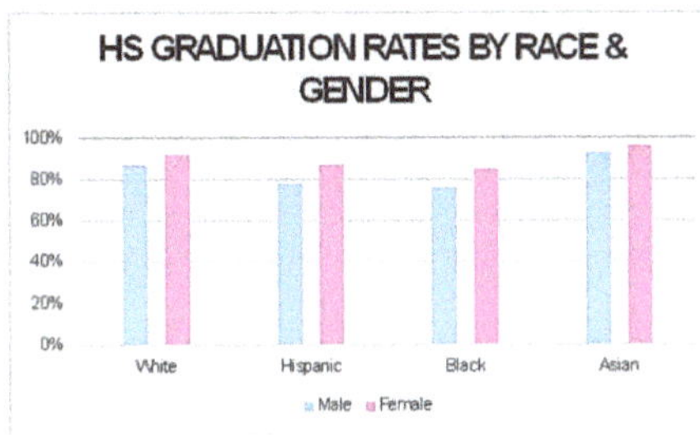

In 2018, nearly 35% of black women held some form of a college degree, compared to just 26.7% of black men. It should also be noted that in one-third of the thirty-eight states surveyed by The Education Trust[3], the college degree attainment gap between black men and women was at least 10% or higher. Degree attainment seems to be lowest in states with higher concentrations of black men. In the Southern states where Black men comprised at least 10% of the population (Mississippi, Louisiana, Georgia, Alabama, and South Carolina), the high school graduation rate for black males was below 55% (Anthony, Jr. , Nichols and Pilar 2021).

I have often witnessed so-called "conscious" or "woke" brothers criticize other black men over education. Recently, I came across a social media post showing a young man returning to his neighborhood following his high school graduation. It was apparent that he was proud of his achievement and wanted to celebrate it with the people in his neighborhood. He would be murdered later that evening while out celebrating this achievement with his friends. I was disappointed to see another black man in the comments of this post suggesting that this young man's murder resulted from his education. To be more specific, his exact comments was, "That's what happens when you are educated by the enemy."

It is difficult enough having to deal with the range of systemic obstacles that often hinder our ability to achieve success outside of the world of sports and entertainment. Enduring the criticism of other black men for simply trying to achieve something more than a life of poverty or crime is beyond insufferable. Apparently, this young man was murdered out of jealously. However, any of us that are actually from urban inner-cities are familiar with this type of jealousy, anger, and aggression that often results from any resemblance of success or achievement.

To be clear, the oldest forms of education in the world find their roots in the fraternities and societies of ancient Africa. In fact, the mysterious brotherhood of Ancient Khemet (which still exists in part today), had spread as far east as Asia and as far west as Southern America thousands of years ago. Many of these mysteries are the subject of modern-day educational concentrations (e.g., medicine, advanced mathematics, Algebra or Al Jabr, astronomy, physics, chemistry or Alchemy or Al Kimiya, and philosophy just to name a few.)

The Absent Black Father

Black men face higher rates of chronic health conditions such as hypertension, diabetes, and heart disease. Access to quality healthcare services, preventive care, and mental health care services is often limited, as most of us do not qualify for subsidized healthcare, due to the fact that we are often denied the innate right and privilege to custody of our children. There is a common misconception within the black community that parent/child relationships are for the sole benefit of the child.

However, both mothers and fathers benefit from healthy relationships with their children.

The human tendency to "rise to the occasions" is a fascinating psychological phenomenon that describes how individuals can perform exceptionally well or demonstrate remarkable courage when faced with challenging situations. This concept highlights our innate ability to adapt and excel under pressure. Whenever you hear someone say, "having my kids slowed down" or "made me grow up." This is the phenomena to which they are alluding. The responsibility of caring for a child is part of the human growth process. By limiting or denying any parent the natural right to contribute to the rearing of their children we are not only depriving that child of their right to a balanced world view, but we are also depriving that parent of their right to evolve into a well-balanced adult.

During antebellum slavery, black men and women were often separated from their children and families. Those of us that were lucky remained within traveling distance and under the authority of a slave owner who would allow them to visit with their children and families on the weekend. However, many were separated to the point of never seeing their families again. Today, we are separated from our children by administrative courts and bitter parents, only entitled to visit with them under court order, and prevented from having any meaningful input into the direction of their lives.

Currently, there is an active effort to push states toward 50/50 custody (there are currently twenty states with 50/50 custody laws)! Even when considering states with 50/50 custody laws, female parents, on average, are granted 65% of custodial time with children. Male parents are granted approximately 35% of custodial time with children. Men, on average, receive about 54% of the custodial time that women are granted (Pedrazas 2021).

Slavery By Another Name

There is disproportionate representation of black men in the trapped in the American criminal justice system. Black men have higher rates of arrest, incarceration, instances of police brutality, and harsher sentencing compared to any other demographic. Across the nation, black men are nearly five times as likely to be incarcerated and 23.4% less likely to receive probation-only sentences compared to white males. Considering the current rate of incarceration, one out of every three black males born today can expect to be sentenced to prison, compared one out of seventeen males (The National Association for the Advancement of Colored People n.d.). According to its 2023 Demographic Differences in Federal Sentencing report, the United State Sentencing Commission[4] reported that black men received 13.4 % longer sentences than while males for the same crimes (United States Sentencing Commission 2023).

Felony conviction can significantly limit employment and career opportunities. Most employers conduct background checks and individuals with serious misdemeanor and felony convictions often face employment discrimination or outright exclusion from certain professions. This often leads to economic instability, including lower wages, irregular employment, and higher rates of poverty compared to their peers without criminal convictions.

There is often a social stigma associated with having a criminal record, which can affect relationships, community standing, and mental well-being. It may also contribute to feelings of isolation or marginalization. Individuals with felony convictions may face challenges reintegrating into society, which can increase the likelihood of recidivism (re-offending and returning to prison). Felony convictions may also result in a loss of certain rights, such as the right to vote, the right to travel to certain countries, and limitations or restrictions to accessing public benefits, financial aid, or housing. Further, formerly incarcerated individuals may experience poorer physical and mental health due to stress, trauma, and lack of access to healthcare services during and after incarceration.

The impact of black men receiving felony convictions and serving time in prison extends beyond the individual. Incarceration can strain family relationships and community ties, affecting children, partners, and broader support networks. The disruption of progress caused by incarceration has long-term social and economic consequences for families and the broader community. For families, this economic hardship often includes difficulty meeting basic needs and increased reliance on social welfare systems. Communities affected by mass incarceration experience economic setbacks as working-age individuals are removed from the workforce (Brennan Center for Justice n.d.).

A Culture of Police Brutality

The origins of modern-day policing can be traced back to "Slave Patrols" during Antebellum Slavery. The earliest formal slave patrol was created in the Carolinas in the early 1700s with one mission: to establish a system of terror and squash slave uprisings with the capacity to pursue, apprehend, and return runaway slaves to their owners. Their tactics included the use of excessive force to control and produce the desired behavior (The National Association for the Advancement of Colored People n.d.). Whit a law enforcement and criminal justice system rooted in slavery; it is no wonder black people encounter police brutality at rates twice that of other groups.

Black people in general are five times more likely than white Americans to be stopped by law enforcement officers without just cause and black men are twice as likely to be stopped than black women. Since 2017, more than eight hundred people have been killed after being pulled over by law enforcement. Tyre Nichols, Jaylen Randle, Philando Castile and countless other black men have been murdered by police during what should have been routine traffic stops. In 2022, traffic stops led to roughly 7% of all police killings nationwide (Debusmann, Jr. 2023).

Since 2005, ninety-eight non-federal law enforcement officers have been arrested in connection with a fatal on-duty shooting. Thirty-five of these officers have been convicted of a crime, often on a lesser offense such as manslaughter or negligent homicide, rather than murder, as in the case of George Floyd. Only three officers that have been convicted of murder during this period have seen their convictions stand. Twenty-two officers have been acquitted in a jury trials and nine have been acquitted during bench trials (The National Association for the Advancement of Colored People n.d.).

In a 2015 National Survey on Drug Use and Health, the Substance Abuse and Mental Health Services Administration reported that about seventeen million white Americans and four million African Americans reported having used an illicit drug within the last month. While black and whites use drugs at similar rates, the imprisonment rate of black Americans for drug related offenses is nearly six times that of whites (Substance Abuse and Mental Health Services Administration 2016).

The Prison Industrial Complex

The prison-industrial complex is a set of interest groups and private prison institutions whose business model is contingent upon incarcerating people. Hundreds of companies benefit from penal labor, including some of America's largest corporations. Wages are equivalent to less than $1 per hour in most penal labor programs, with up to 12-hour workdays. The pay scale for federal prisoners is $.12 to $.40 per hour. In certain states, such as Texas, inmates are not paid for labor. Nevertheless, the Texas penal labor system, managed by Texas Correctional Industries, was valued at $88.9 million in 2014. The estimated annual value of prison and jail industrial output is $2 billion.

A Culture of Violence

I cannot in good conscious tell black men to put down the weapons. Yet, it is imperative that we learn to resolve conflict, especially among each other, without immediately resorting to violence. Taking a human life should only ever be considered under the most extreme of circumstances, such as protecting another human life or the sanctity of our women and children. Nevertheless, I overstand the environment in which many of us live. I know from first-hand experience, that regardless of whether I have actually committed some atrocity that warrants an act of violence, I have to diligently protect my life and that of my family from those outside of my community who would want to wish me harm simply based on my ethnicity, beliefs, or political views and from other black men and women for any number of trivial reason such as the lyrics of a song, facial expressions, or the women I am dating. Now is definitely not the time to put down your weapons!

Black men are often loyal to a fault! Not that there is anything dishonorable about loyalty. The problem is that our loyalties are often misplaced. We choose loyalty to our friends over the future and well-being of our families and children. Young black men would rather spend 50 years in prison that turn their back on their friends. The same friends that would not put $25 on your books for commissary nor buy your child a Christmas gift while you were incarcerated. The same friends who would easily turn their back on you at the first sign of trouble. It took me living on the streets with my mother, literally sleeping in the back of our vehicle, to realize that most of the people I had given my loyalty, did not even deserve my friendship. Who are they to even expect, let alone demand loyalty?

A Clever Deception

According to its most recent report on median weekly earning by gender and race, the Bureau of Labor Statistics reported that in 2023 there were

8.5 million black women in the labor force compared to 7.9 million black men. The median weekly earnings for black men were approximately $970.00 compared to $889.00 for black women. Implicitly that means that for every $1.00 that enters the African American community, $0.52 in earned by men and $0.48 is earned by women.

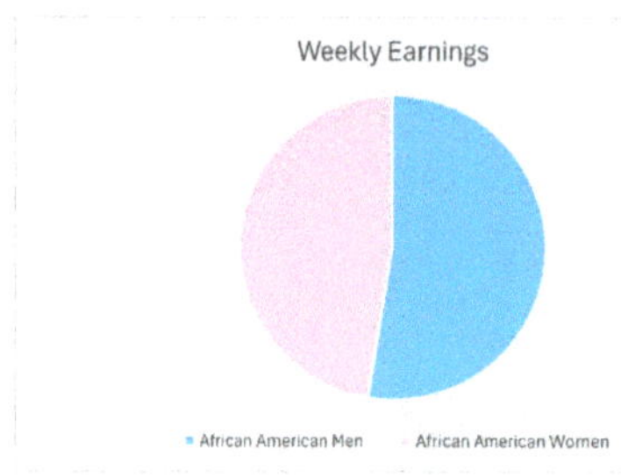

For the past several years we have been bombarded with messaging regarding 'disparity in pay' by gender, especially as it relates to black women. What I have noticed is that although the median income for African American men is slightly higher than African American women the messaging is always based on the comparison of black women to white men, who on average earn more than any other demographic with the possible exception of Asian men. Yet, the 'disparity in pay' narrative is always "men" in general, not white men in particular.

The disparity in weekly earnings between African American men and African American women results partially from a smaller sample size (as there are generally fewer black men with gainful employment due, in party, to several of the factors discussed in this section. In smaller samples, outliers have a greater impact on the overall average. In larger samples, the voluminous data points stabilize averages and other statistical estimates, making them more representative of the general population[5]. Likewise, for years men, in generally, have worked unskilled high-paying occupations traditionally reserved for men (trucking, construction, O&G, etc.) However, there are in fact, a few exceptionally high-earning African American men that when combined with the small sample size skew an otherwise normal distribution.

Regardless of the reasons for the 'disparity in pay' between African American men and African American women, what this narrative does not consider is disposable income. Even after a noticeable decrease over the past two decades, one in five custodial parents are women and half of all custodial parents had either legal or informal child support agreements in place with at least half (58%) receiving some type of non cash support (SNAP, housing, subsidized health care, etc.). None of which is counted as income nor taxed for custodial parents who are often women (Grall 2020).

Allow me to explain the implication! Let us suppose that we have an unmarried father in the State of Texas that earns $970.00 a week and an unmarried mother that earns $889.00 a week. Shortly after the birth of that child, the mother is contacted by the Department of Health & Human Services informing her that she and the child are eligible for government subsidized health insurance. She and the child are eligible for this service regardless of whether the father has that child on a privately funded health insurance plan. The unmarried mother is also eligible for SNAP, housing, and several other public benefits.

If either the unmarried mother or the child is enrolled in any of these benefits programs, the child becomes a ward of the state, the unwed mother becomes the assignor (assignor of her rights over the child), and the unwed farther is placed on title IV child support. In the state of Texas, a noncustodial father earning $970.00 a week must $177.14 post tax dollars a week in child support to the custodial mother, effectively reducing his gross pay to $792.86 and increasing the custodial mother's gross pay to $1,066.

Cashflows	Noncustodial	Custodial	Notes
Earnings	$970.00	$889.00	
Child Support	($177.14)	$177.14	Not taxable
SNAP	Ineligible	$129.00	Not taxable.
Section 8	Ineligible	250	Not taxable.
Net Cash	792.86	1006.14	
Value	$792.86	$1,385.14	+(592.28)

Disposable Income

Once you begin to consider the benefits associated with child custody it becomes apparent that although African American women earn slightly less than African American men on "average" their disposable income is much greater, nearly $30,000 a year greater in the example above. I would also like to highlight the fact that the unmarried father's $792.86 of incoming cash flow will be taxed at $970.00, further reducing his disposable income. Child support and many of these "public" benefits are simply a method for transferring wealth out of the black communities in general and black men in particular. I am not saying that black women have it easy. I am saying that there is an active effort to place and keep black men at the bottom of the social ladder.

As a demographic, we are unable to combat these types of systemic challenges because we are giving away our individual right to vote and our collective voting power. Every time a young black man becomes entangled in the criminal justice system, we are dug a little deeper into this hole. Every time a black man is gunned down in the street, we lose what could have been a doctor, lawyer, scientist, or even the average joe that one day might have saved your life. This culture of violence and aggression among black men just makes it easier for the world to turn its backs on us as we unknowingly march toward the gallows. We cannot expect anyone to save us from this situation that we may not have created, but we have definitely perpetuated, especially when it benefits them. We cannot depend on the Barack Obama's of the world, black women, and in some cases not even other black men.

I would encourage my brothers to take note to the fact that it is becoming increasingly difficult to find objective statistics that measure factors across gender and race as they relate to African American men. My fear is that this is by design and alludes to an earlier statement in this book regarding the scientific insignificance of race. As stated by William "Lord Kelvin" Thompson, "if you cannot measure it, you cannot improve it." How can we hope to gauge our progress and further improve upon the state of our community, if there is no information against which to measure our performance? How can one hope to reason, without accurate knowledge and information on which to base our assumptions?

Black Men and Nuwaubu

Black men often confront negative stereotypes and societal prejudices that affect their opportunities in employment, education, and social interactions. These stereotypes can also impact their mental health and well-being. Structural challenges such as father absence, separation from children, family instability, and community violence contribute to social and economic pressures on African American men and their families. Despite efforts towards political empowerment, black men still face obstacles in exercising their voting rights and participating in civic life.

However, every day above ground is an opportunity for change! I know that at times it seems like the more you try to do right, the harder life becomes. My suspicion is that the universe is testing us, to reveal to inner selves the true motives of our actions. Are we doing right because we expect some reward or temporary relief from a reality that we have created for ourselves out of ignorance? Or are we trying to do right simply because it is the right thing to do?

Nuwaubu, as the philosophical science of Sound Right Reason, encompasses various principles and teachings that could potentially benefit black men facing the challenges outlined in this chapter. Nuwaubu emphasizes reconnecting with African cultural roots and heritage which can empower black men by fostering a keen sense of identity and pride in their ancestry, thereby counteracting negative stereotypes and societal prejudices.

Nuwaubu places a high importance on knowledge acquisition, including ancient wisdom and formal education. Encouraging African American men to pursue education, not only in western academics but also in cultural and historical studies, can uplift their self-worth and provide them with tools needed to navigate systemic inequalities. Nuwaubu promotes spiritual growth and mental clarity through practices that focus on self-awareness, inner peace, and mindfulness that can help black men cope with stress, trauma, and societal pressures thereby promoting mental well-being.

The Culture of Nuwaubu emphasizes the importance of community support and brotherhood, encouraging African American men to build supportive networks within their communities. These networks can provide them with resources, mentorship, and solidarity needed to overcome challenges like unemployment, incarceration, and social stigmatization. Nuwaubu also supports the principles of social justice and activism by educating black men about systemic injustices and empowering them to advocate for change. Nuwaubu can help address issues such as disparities in education and economic inequalities by offering a holistic approach that integrates cultural awareness, education, spiritual growth, community support, activism, and family values. By embracing these principles, African American men can potentially find empowerment, resilience, and a path toward improving their individual circumstances and contributing positively to their communities.

[1] A stratum is the group of elements that have been integrated to others in the formation of the language. [2] The Brookings Institution is a nonprofit organization based in Washington, D.C., who conducts in-depth nonpartisan research to improve policy and local, national, and global governance. [3] The Education Trust, Inc, is a nonprofit organization based out of Washington, D.C., committed to advancing policies and practices to dismantle the racial and economic barriers embedded in the American education system. [4] The U.S. Sentencing Commission is a bipartisan, independent agency located in the judicial branch of the government. It was created by Congress in 1984 to reduce sentencing disparities and promote transparency and proportionality in sentencing. [5] For more information on the impact of outliers on smaller samples sizes in representative statistical analysis please read Sample Size Essentials at Statistics by Jim https://statisticsbyjim.com.

8

Who are Nuwaubians?

At the onset of our journey, I emphasized the necessity of grasping the concept of Nuwaubu to truly comprehend the identity of Nuwaubians. It is my sincerest hope that by now you have developed a deeper overstanding of the Philosophical Science of Nuwaubu. Nevertheless, the notion of Nuwaubu transcends mere philosophy; it encompasses language, a cultural ethos, and PEOPLE! Nuwaubians are persons of color; born in the Americas, descendant of the original inhabitants of the continent known to us today as Africa, who through centuries of ethnic oppression and cultural suppression, are no longer able to identify with any individual modern tribe of the continent. Nuwaubians are by definition what is known today as African Americans.

I first encountered the teachings of Malachi Z. York in the Summer of 1997. I can easily remember this period in my life as I can vividly recall the presence of what is known to us today as the Hale-Bopp comet. Over the past 27 years I have interacted with many Nuwaubians from numerous backgrounds and on various paths in life. Being from a small city in the Bible Belt South, I have encountered Nuwaubians of the various forms of Christianity, from Southern Baptist to the Pan African Orthodox. I have also encountered many Nuwaubians of the various forms of Islam, from the Nation of Islam to the Moorish Science Temple of America. I have encountered Nuwaubian of the many forms of Judaism, Buddhist, Sikhs, Panthers, Cherokee, Choctaw, Yamassee, whatever! What these groups all have in common is the same thing that separates them. They are all in search of a genuine and authentic identity.

During the Transatlantic Slave Trade, upon arriving in the Americas, our people were subjected to an acclimation process known as 'seasoning'. Seasoning, often taking place over the course of several years, adjusted the newly arrived captives to the ecology of the western hemisphere and the social environment of the Americas. This process involved destroying any notions of affinity with their past lives, breaking their individual and collective will to resist, and physiological adaptation to the system of slavery. African captives were forced into extreme working and living conditions, often succumbing to diseases such as hypoascorbemia, amoebic dysentery, smallpox, measles, and influenza during their first few years in captivity. Death rates differed throughout the Americas reaching as high as 50% in thirteen colonies (Stephens 2010). Our prior faiths, languages, and customs were prohibited and often addressed by brute force.

Race & Ethnic Identity

Since the first captives arrived at the shores of America, we have been searching to restore our stolen identities. Identity can be defined as the set of characteristics by which a person or thing is definitively recognizable or know. Despite the diversity of civilizations from which we originated, once here we were homogenized into a single, overarching racial category, primarily defined by skin color. The mainstream belief among scientists today is that race has no genetic or scientific basis and is purely a social construct used to establish and justify systems of power, privilege, disenfranchisement, and oppression. However, the idea of race as a social construct is not new. This concept was first introduced into American society by W.E.B. Dubois in his 28-page essay 'The Conversation of Race'. Du Bois was concerned that race was being used as a biological explanation for what he understood to be social and cultural differences between two populations of people. He spoke out against the idea of "white" and "black" as discrete groups, claiming that these distinctions ignored the scope of human diversity. What scientists are now coming to understand is that while a person's skin color may be superficial and seem to possess no scientific or biological significance, race (as in racial identity) and skin color are altogether two separate notions. One cannot necessarily determine a person's racial identity by skin color alone! Such is the case with many Albino people of color.

The truth of the matter is that the term "race," as in skin color, is insufficient at describing the components that constitute a shared racial identity. Racial identity, or Ethnicity as a more appropriate choice of words, is a term used to describe how we perceive ourselves and how others perceive us with respect to race &/or ethnicity. Ethnicity specifically refers to ethnic traits (including skin tone, eye color, hair texture), constitution, background, association, or affiliations. Prior to the enslavement of our ancestors, what distinguished one group of African people from another was culture (art, beliefs, customs, institutions, religion, etc.). Nevertheless, even as a purely social construct, the concept of racial identity is scientific in nature. Science, by definition, is the systematic study of the structure and behavior of the physical and natural world through observation, experiment, and testing of theories against the evidence obtained.

Ethnic Identity development is defined as "the process in which humans develop a clear and unique view of their identity as it relates to (an) ethnic group(s). Ethnic identity is characterized as part of one's overarching self-concept and identification. Ethnic identity development is a crucial aspect of overall identity formation, encompassing how individuals understand and relate to their ethnic or cultural heritage. This process often begins in childhood and continues throughout life, shaped by individual experiences, family dynamics, societal influences, and cultural practices.

During childhood, ethnic identity development typically begins with awareness of one's ethnic background through family traditions, language, and cultural celebrations. As individuals grow older their interactions with peers, media representation, and educational experiences play significant roles in shaping their understanding of their ethnic identity. This phase often involves exploring and internalizing cultural values, beliefs, and practices, which may differ from mainstream cultural norms.

Adolescence marks a critical period for ethnic identity formation, as individuals navigate questions of belonging, discrimination, and cultural pride. Adolescents may actively seek to understand their ethnic identity by exploring cultural history, participating in community events, or engaging with peers from similar backgrounds. This exploration helps shape a sense of belonging and provides a framework for understanding how ethnicity intersects with other aspects of identity, such as gender, socioeconomic status, and personal aspirations.

In adulthood, ethnic identity continues to evolve through life experiences, relationships, and broader societal changes. Adults may negotiate their ethnic identity in various contexts, balancing cultural heritage with professional roles, societal expectations, and personal relationships. This ongoing development can lead to a deeper appreciation of cultural diversity, resilience in the face of discrimination, and a sense of responsibility towards preserving and promoting one's ethnic heritage for future generations. Overall, ethnic identity development is a dynamic process that reflects an individual's evolving understanding of self and connection to their cultural roots.

We cannot hope to put an end to racism by ignoring the ethnic identity of millions of people of color displaced throughout the world. Why must we deny ourselves and our children the rich inheritance of our ancestry because of the myopia of America's racist past? To suggest race as purely a social construct and without significance would be to abate the long suffering of our ancestors and to diminish the significance of their contributions to civilization. To this very day mainstream American society is still attempting to reduce us to a color, a derogatory term, and a conquered people. As of this writing there is a push my right-wing conservatives to write us out of U.S. history due to their own guilt and fear. What our ancestors knew and what many white Americans are beginning to realize is that there is far more shame in being the descendant of a slave owner than being the descendant of a slave!

The Black Identity Crisis

An 'ethnic group' regards itself or is regarded by others as a distinct community by virtue of certain characteristics that help to distinguish it from the surrounding community. As it regards Nuwaubian people, our racial identities, languages, religions, and traditions have largely been imposed upon us by dominant western cultures. Within the Christian community we are African American. In the Nation of Islam, we are the Lost Tribe of Shabazz. In the community of Black Hebrew Israelites, we are Hebrew, Chosen of Y'srael. To the Moorish Science Temple, we are the Moors of northern 'Africa'. For some, we are the various indigenous tribes of North America. In all cases, we are supposedly from a Land, culture, or religion that is dominated by a people other than our own, who either refuse to acknowledge and accept us or are incapable of assisting us in restoring our sense of dignity and self-worth. A genuine ethnic identity is not created for, nor enforced upon, you by an abusive dominant culture. It is instinctive, autogenous, and does not result from restrictions imposed upon you by your oppressor.

The word Negro is a term previously used to identify People of Color. According the Farlex, Inc., Free Online Dictionary, a Negro is any member of the "Negroid" race and may be distinguished by physical characteristics such as brown or black skin, tightly curled hair, and includes people indigenous to sub-Saharan 'Africa'. Although the terms Negro and Negroid are no longer in scientific use, the term was coined as a scientific racial categorization in the 1800s. The term black, as it relates to racial classifications, is defined as an "American" ethnic group descended from "African" people having dark skin. The progressive term "African American" is defined as "A black American of African Ancestry." Note that the word black is not capitalized and implies that the term black, as it is used above, denotes a color of the visual light spectrum and has absolutely nothing to do with race or ethnicity. As eloquently stated by our 44th President Mr. Barack H. Obama "Black has no standing at law."

Our Moorish brothers and sisters often point to the following noteworthy hypothesis as evidence to support the adoption of the term Moor as our true ethnic identity. It is supposed that the term Africa originated from Roman general and consul Scipio Africanus who invaded and perpetuated war on the continent known today to us as 'Africa'. It is true, Africa may in fact be named after a hostile Roman invader. Nevertheless, this does not justify Moor as our true historical identity. The term Moor denotes membership to a specific, traditionally Muslim, society of a mixed Berber (Berber is a Greek word for Barbarian and was used to describe members of a particular ethnic group indigenous to what is now northwest Africa) and Arab ancestry. This is supported by the Spanish etymology of the word Moor. The Strait of Gibraltar which separates Spain and Morocco is only ten miles across. You can literally see Spain from Dalia Beach in Morocco. Nevertheless, Moors only constitute a small part of our ethnic heritage and applies specifically to the mixed Berber and Arab Muslim community of northwest Africa. This pattern of ethnic stratum is not exclusive to Nuwaubian people. Today, we refer to the indigenous population of America by various names such as Indian, Hispanic, or Latin. However, Spanish, and Spanish people are European. Latin is an Indo-European language spoken in ancient Rome. Obviously, Indian people are from India!

Today, we are largely without a distinct collective identity separate and apart from the racial and social narrative created for us by a dominant

American society that has historically been indifferent to our suffering. Those among us who have chosen to reject the restraints of social colonialism often find themselves in the position of adopting or mimicking identities and cultures dominated by those with whom we share no recognizable kinship. Our holidays, holy days, heroes, villains, language, even our names are all sanctioned to us by the broader American society. For most Nuwaubian, our holidays and holy days consist of Christmas, Thanksgiving, Easter, New Year, Independence Day, Memorial Day, Labor Day, Mother's Day, Father's Day, Halloween, and Valentines Day. None of which, with the possible exception of Memorial Day and now Juneteenth have anything to do with "African Americans"[1].

Our lack of a collective ethnic identity, cultural heritage, and history that honors human dignity has plunged "black" America into a widespread identity crisis. This predicament is only exacerbated by the derogatory, often self-perpetuating, identity imposed on us by the broader Eurocentric American culture. Systemic racism, indifference, the privatization of criminal justice, racial terrorism, political violence, and covert government operations such as the FBI's COINTEL Pro or the CIA's IRAN Contra Scandal all work in concerted effort to undermine the African American community's ability to fulfill their broader roles as Americans.

The Ethnogenesis of Nuwaubu

In all earnest, enslaved people originated from a diversity of religious backgrounds, regions, cultures, kingdoms, and queendoms across the African continent. It is unlikely that any of us, who are descended from America's formerly enslaved population, can assert a genetic connection to any specific group of the Africa continent with a certainty of at least 50% (The National Library of Medicine| The National Center for Biotechnology Information 2009). This disconnection from our ethnic roots has left a void that many have sought to fill through various means, including the exploration and adoption of essentially foreign cultural practices and identities that resonate with them individually or the acceptance of the historical and cultural narrative created for us by the broader American society. Indeed, the transatlantic slave trade disrupted and obscured the specific ethnic, cultural, and religious origins of millions of Africans, forcibly integrating them into a new ethnic and social construct with a distinct identity shaped by centuries of slavery, segregation, and systemic racism.

Nuwaubu encapsulates the essence of an ethnic identity, embodying the cultural, social, and physiological attributes that distinguish Nuwaubians from the broader mosaic of American society. These attributes encompass not only physical traits traditionally associated with race —complexion, hair texture, and ancestral lineage—but also the social and cultural signifiers like language & dialect, social status, and systems of belief. Furthermore, the rich heritage of Nuwaubu includes culinary traditions, attire, and artistic expressions that are integral to the Nuwaubian identity. The term ethnicity is often used interchangeably with 'nation', particularly as it relates to a collective bound by shared customs, core values, and language. The overlap is especially pronounced in the context of ethnic nationalism. For the Nuwaubian community, ethnicity is both an inheritance and a societal imposition, the duality of which frames our place within the American narrative. Nuwaubians may be further divided into subgroups or tribes such as Moor (Nuwaubian Moor or Moorish Science Temple of America), Shabazz (Nation of Islam), or Nazarene (Various forms of Christianity) which underscores the dynamic nature of Nuwaubian ethnicity and highlights the intricate process of ethnogenesis that shapes our unique position in the historical and cultural context of America.

We need only revisit our definition of Nuwaubian to conceptualize its ethnogenesis. As previously defined, a Nuwaubian is a person of color; born in the Americas, descended from the original inhabitants of the continent known to us today as Africa, who through centuries of ethnic and cultural suppression, are no longer able to identify with any modern tribe of continent. The physical characteristics of a Nuwaubian are all but obvious, a broad array of hues, wavy to woolly hair, prominent eye color and physical stature. Our common origins, ancestry, history, social status, and the way we practice our chosen system of belief reflect a fraternal bond that has endured the most distressing trials of the human family. Yet, the robustness of our cultural legacy, vibrant style of dress, flavorful cuisine, rich traditions, and emotive forms of art speaks to the tenacity of our people.

Ethnic Boundaries

Our various identities, of which ethnicity is but a part, intersect to form the complex nexus of unique living experiences. Some of these experiences are shared, simultaneously creating solidarity within the group and ethnic boundaries without. According to Norwegian social anthropologist Frederik Barth, ethnic boundaries are cognitive or mental boundaries situated in the minds of people and are the result of the collective efforts of construction and maintenance. So too are governments, civilizations, and relationships! All of which are conceptual in nature, nevertheless manifesting pragmatic consequences. Frederik Barth sought to quash the idea of cultures as bounded entities and advocated the decoupling of distinct ethnic groups. I can only assume that Dr. Barth's intentions were honorable. Yet, his approach lacks respect for the history, heritage, and culture of the same ethnic minorities it sought to protect. Our racial and ethnic identities are often viewed in relation to their similarities or differences from others. It is true that ethnic boundaries can reinforce negative stereotypes and perpetuate situations in which ethnic minorities are viewed as rivals by dominant groups. However, not all ethnic boundaries are harmful. Ethnic boundaries also serve to define and unite cultural groups, fostering a sense of solidarity and belonging through shared customs, heritage, and celebrations. It is through ethnic boundaries that members of ethnic communities establish unique identities. The problem is not ethnic boundaries, it is a lack of respect.

Ethnicity plays a crucial role in shaping individuals' overall sense of self. As a form of social identity, ethnicity reflects our personal commitment to specific social groups, characterized by shared cultural customs, religious practices, geographic origins, and historical experiences. Unfortunately, ethnic boundaries are used by some as a basis for discrimination, leading to practices like police brutality and racial discrimination. Some ethnic identities are fluid and subject to change, influenced by factors such as globalization and acculturation. This fluidity gives rise to hybrid identities, where individuals may blend aspects of different ethnicities or adapt their identities in response to diverse cultural influences.

The Importance of a Shared Ethnic Identity

The onus is not on 'America' to forge for us a respectable ethnic identity, culture, and heritage. However, our situation has led to the creation of a new, syncretic identity that, while not tied to a single African culture, reflects the shared history, struggles, and resilience of a particular group of African people. Nuwaubu is the result our desire to forge an identity that honors our African roots while acknowledging the unique cultural developments that have occurred in the diaspora. The culture, language, and science of Nuwaubu emphasize the importance of self-definition and the rejection of identities and values imposed by a historically oppressive society.

For many Nuwaubians, race &/or ethnicity plays a significant role in our daily lives. It often influences our experiences, determines the extent of our opportunities, presents certain risk, shapes our self-perceptions, and the way that others perceive us. In 2019 the Pew Research Center published, Race in America 2019, a comprehensive study into the way we as Americans view race relations, racial inequality, and the role of race and ethnicity in our personal lives. Unsurprisingly, the study suggest that the American public has negative views of the country's racial progress. Discrimination remains a pervasive issue in American society, with a considerable proportion of black and Asian individuals reporting experiences of unfair treatment due to their race. This includes being subject to suspicion, stereotypes of intelligence, and outright racial slurs and jokes. More than half of the respondents suggested that America's 45th president, Donald J. Trump, has worsened race relations in this country. The report also revealed that Nuwaubians, more than any other ethnicity, tend to view race and ethnicity as more central to their individual identities. Nearly three-quarters (74%) of Nuwaubian respondents say being "black" is either extremely, or at least especially important, to how they view themselves (Horowitz, Brown and Cox 2019).

Ethnic pride describes the positive feelings that result from membership in one or more ethnic groups. Ethnic pride is a source of self-respect and dignity and is often characterized by an appreciation and understanding of one's culture and history. It does not involve arrogant, racist, or ethnocentric aggression. Ethnocentrism refers to discrimination against other ethnic cultures due to a belief in the superiority of our own. For Nuwaubian people a high degree of ethnic pride has been discouraged, instead emphasizing acculturation and assimilation into the broader Eurocentric American culture. Despite these pressures we have managed to preserve some sense of self and kind. Our custom hairstyles and dress, the ways in which we have practiced religions traditionally foreign to our ancestors, and the ways we have adapted the American diet are all evidence of the possibility of having a high (or low) degree of ethnic pride and also being more (or less) acculturated to mainstream American society.

Increasing ethnic pride among Nuwaubian people involves engaging in activities that celebrate and cultivate positive attitudes toward our diverse subcultures and tribes. Exposure to a broad spectrum of ethnic role models, beyond those deemed acceptable by the prevailing American norms, alongside educational resources such as books and films, travel, and participation in cultural festivities—ranging from ethnic cuisines to music and dancing—serve as vital avenues for fostering this pride. Research indicates that individuals with heightened levels of ethnic pride exhibit better overall health, achieve higher academic success, and show lower tendencies towards substance abuse. Thus, fostering ethnic pride within the Nuwaubian community not only strengthens our collective identity but also contributes significantly to the well-being and advancement of our people.

However, the ability and responsibility to celebrate our ethnic diversity while avoiding racism and ethnocentrism has never been more important. The delicate balance between racial/ethnic pride and racism/ethnocentrism, which is crucial to fostering a society where differences are celebrated without undermining peace, is under threat by increasing tendencies to discriminate and segregate based on our racial and ethnic differences. We must draw a clear distinction between ethnic and racial pride as a source of dignity versus a catalyst for division and discrimination.

[1] It is supposed by some that Memorial Day originated from Nuwaubian people in Jackson, MS in 1865 in which 10,000 people celebrated the life and death of 257 dead Union soldiers. Gardiner, Richard; Jones, P. Michael; Bellware, Daniel (Spring–Summer 2018). "The Emergence and Evolution of Memorial Day". *Journal of America's Military Past*. 43–2 (137): 19–37. Retrieved May 25, 2020.)

9

What is Nuwaubian Culture?

The first anthropological definition of culture was crafted in 1871 by British anthropologist Sir. Edward Burnett Tylor. As defined by Sir Edward, Culture or Civilization, taken in its wide ethnographic sense, is that complex whole which includes knowledge, beliefs, art, morals, law, customs, and any other capabilities and habits acquired by mankind as a member of a society. Ethnography simply refers to the scientific description of peoples and cultures with their customs, habits, and mutual differences. For example, I Am Nuwaubian is an ethnographic book on Nuwaubian people in America. Over the past century and a half, the meaning of culture has evolved to take on multiple definitions. For the purpose of this book, we will retain the use of Sir. Edward Burnett Tylor's original anthropological definition of culture.

The Culture of Nuwaubu

If you were previously familiar with Nuwaubians you may think that our culture centers around secret/sacred orders, Egyptian styled dress and art, tall black Fez's, or even a cultish styled leader currently serving a 135-year prison sentence in a Federal Administrative Super-Maximum-Security Facility in Florence, Colorado. You are correct, the culture of Nuwaubu is all of these things and more. Reflecting on our definition of Nuwaubian, it must naturally follow that Nuwaubian Culture is that complex whole which includes the knowledge, beliefs, art, morals, law, customs and any other capabilities and habits acquired by a person of color; born in the American who through centuries of ethnic oppression and cultural suppression, are no longer able to identify with any modern tribe of the continent. Thus, the Harlem Renaissance, Black Art, the Black Power Movement, the Civil Rights Movement, Black is Beautiful, Black Lives Matter, Creole, Geechie, Caribbean, Hattian, Afros, Cornrows, Dreadlocks, Jazz, Swing, Ragtime, Blues, R&B and Hip Hop are all Nuwaubian culture. Should you choose to identify as Nuwaubian, allowing anyone to tell you otherwise would be the same as allowing someone to tell you that you are not black.

The Harlem Renaissance

Nuwaubian Culture is not wholly distinct from the broader American culture. Many of our traditions, customs, beliefs, cuisine, art, music, education, knowledge, and especially our languages have been influenced by either a forced adhesion or exclusion from many aspects of western life by the dominant ruling classes. The Harlem Renaissance, spanning throughout the 1920s and 30s, is widely recognized as first "African American" cultural, social, and artistic explosion accepted by the broader American society. It marked a period where Nuwaubian music, literature, art, and theater flourished, making significant contributions to American culture and society at large. Although the Harlem Renaissance was centered in the Harlem neighborhood of New York City, its influence spread across the United States and even internationally. The Harlem Renaissance was birthed out of the harsh realities of life in the early 20th century, including racial segregation, the Great Migration, and the search for a collective identity and self-expression.

Figures like Langston Hughes, Zora Neale Hurston, and Claude McKay used poetry and prose to express the complexities of Nuwaubian life, blending themes of racial pride, economic struggles, and resistance against racial injustice. Their works challenged stereotypes and offered a new, empowered narrative for the 'black' identity.

Jazz and blues, rooted in African traditions, became the soundtrack of the Harlem Renaissance. Musicians like Duke Ellington and Louis Armstrong brought these genres to the forefront of American entertainment, influencing generations of musicians to come. These genres were pivotal in breaking down racial barriers in the music industry and fostering an appreciation for the musical contributions of Nuwaubian people.

Artists such as Aaron Douglas and Jacob Lawrence depicted the black experience, often incorporating African elements into their work. Their art challenged racial stereotypes and celebrated Nuwaubian heritage, contributing to a broader understanding and appreciation of Nuwaubian aesthetics and narratives. The Harlem Renaissance was also a golden age for Nuwaubian theater and performance, with figures like Josephine Baker gaining international fame. The Cotton Club and the Apollo Theater became iconic venues that showcased Nuwaubian talent, breaking new ground for black entertainers.

The Civil Rights & Black Power Movements

The Civil Rights Movement focused on ending segregation and discrimination against black people, primarily through legal and nonviolent means. Leaders like Dr. Martin Luther King Jr., Rosa Parks, and organizations such as the NAACP (National Association for the Advancement of Colored People) played significant roles in this movement. Key achievements of the Civil Rights Movement included the Brown v. Board of Education Supreme Court decision (1954), the Civil Rights Act of 1964, and the Voting Rights Act of 1965. The movement profoundly influenced Nuwaubian culture, fostering a sense of unity, pride, and resilience. It also inspired a rich body of literature, music, and art that reflected the struggles, hopes, and aspirations of Nuwaubians fighting for equality in America. Songs like "We Shall Overcome" became anthems of the movement, embodying the collective struggle for justice. The Civil Rights Movement received mixed reactions from mainstream American society. In the South, where segregation was deeply entrenched, resistance to desegregation was fierce, often resulting in violence against activists. However, the movement also garnered significant support from some segments of the white population, particularly among those in the North and progressive communities who were sympathetic to the cause of racial justice. The movement's nonviolent approach and moral clarity helped sway public opinion over time, contributing to the passage of landmark civil rights legislation.

Emerging in the mid-1960s as a result of the violence perpetrated against Civil Rights activist, the Black Power Movement represented a more militant and radical approach to racial equality, emphasizing racial pride, economic empowerment, and the creation of political and cultural institutions for Nuwaubian people. Figures like Malcolm X, Stokely Carmichael (Kwame Ture), and organizations like the Black Panther Party were central to the Black Power Movement. The movement also embraced African heritage, influencing fashion, music, and art, with Afrocentric styles becoming symbols of empowerment. The Black Power Movement had a significant impact on Nuwaubian culture, encouraging a reevaluation of Nuwaubian identity and heritage. It inspired a generation to embrace their African roots, leading to a surge in African-inspired names, clothing, and artistic expressions. This movement also played a crucial role in developing community programs, such as free breakfast for children and free healthcare clinics, showcasing a commitment to community betterment.

The Black Power Movement was often viewed with suspicion and hostility by white Americans, particularly in the South. Its militant stance and calls for radical change were perceived as a threat to the existing social order. The movement was frequently met with aggressive law enforcement responses, and media portrayals often emphasized its most confrontational aspects, overshadowing its community service initiatives and efforts to build Nuwaubian economic and political power. In both the Civil Rights and Black Power movements, the South represented the stronghold of resistance, where the push for racial equality challenged the deeply rooted social and economic structures of segregation. The reactions of white Southerners ranged from violent opposition to reluctant acceptance of change influenced by national pressure and evolving legal standards. Overall, the Civil Rights and Black Power movements left an indelible mark on American culture, reshaping the nation's understanding of racial equality and justice. While they faced significant resistance, these movements succeeded in mobilizing public opinion and effecting legislative changes, contributing to the gradual transformation of societal attitudes toward race and equality in the United States.

Nuwaubian Literature

Nuwaubian Literature is a rich tapestry of the historical, emotional, and cultural experiences of Nuwaubian people as we have navigated our course through racism, slavery, poverty, drugs, mass incarceration, and police brutality. Its origins lie deep in the oral traditions of enslaved Africans striving for freedom in America. Nuwaubian Literature has provided the average white American and the rest of the world with first-hand accounts of the oppression, trauma, and violence associated with American slavery. It has also been instrumental in dismantling the barriers of inequality, discrimination, and stereotypes (Windsor 2022).

The roots of Nuwaubian literature can be traced back to the 18th century Slave Narratives of Phillis Wheatley and Olaudah Equiano, whose works serve as the inaugural cornerstone of this pivotal heritage. Their vivid legacy was followed by the works Frederick Douglass, Harriet Jacobs, and a host of unsung visionaries, whose riveting narratives traversed the depths of their individual experiences. American Slave Narratives have served as an instrumental catalyst in propelling abolition, offering first-hand accounts of slavery, its profound repercussions on the human spirit, and its overarching implications on pivotal historical phenomena such as the Civil War and the Underground Railroad. Over time, slave narratives have evolved beyond their primary presences as autobiographies and enunciated histories. They have breathed life into a diverse literary genre encompassing not only historical manuscripts and real-time accounts but also an expansive spectrum of fictional works.

The trajectory of Nuwaubian literature has been largely influenced by the shifting dynamics of our role within the broader American society. Since the Reconstruction era, Nuwaubian scribes have traversed an extensive spectrum of thematic terrains. They have probed profoundly into the vast depths of racial identity, institutional racism, and segregation, all the while illuminating the fore with fascinating explorations into the realms of science fiction, fantasy, and romance. Key among these are the works of W.E.B. Du Bois and Booker T. Washington, who vehemently held divergent views as to the proper course for the newly emancipated Nuwaubian people.

The Harlem Renaissance was also instrumental in the development of Nuwaubian literature, profoundly shifting its landscape and catalyzing its progression. Acclaimed authors, poets, and thinkers of the period utilized literature as a medium through which they could articulate the intricacies of their identities, experiences, and perspectives. One of the foremost writers of the era was Langston Hughes, whose masterful blending of colloquial language with elements of blues and jazz music pioneered the innovation of 'Jazz Poetry'. His works, such as "The Negro Speaks of Rivers" and "I, too", not only presented a vivid portrayal of Nuwaubian history and the 'black' experience but also resonated with the aspirations and discontents of everyday Americans. Similarly, Zora Neale Hurston's literary genius was evident in novels like "Their Eyes Were Watching God." In contrast to many of her contemporaries, Hurston did not exclusively focus on the racial injustices against Nuwaubians but celebrated the richness and strength of Nuwaubian culture and vernacular. Through vibrant characters and portrayals of love, identity, and personal growth, her writings breathed much-needed life into elements of Nuwaubian culture often dismissed by mainstream society.

Authors of the Harlem Renaissance, such as Claude McKay, Jean Toomer, and Countee Cullen explored and redefined the parameters of Nuwaubian identity and experience in America. Their literary works offered a platform for visibility and respect for the multiplicity of Nuwaubian experiences. The Harlem Renaissance introduced the concept of the "New Negro," which underscored self-reliance, racial pride, intellectual and artistic excellence while advocating for civil and political rights.

It was a period that helped to redefine how America, and indeed the world, viewed black people. The artistic, intellectual, and cultural explosion during the Harlem Renaissance promoted Nuwaubian self-expression, fostered racial pride, and laid the groundwork for future waves of black literary and cultural assertion. The contributions from the Harlem Renaissance signaled an immensely transformative era in the evolution of Nuwaubian literature, challenging prevailing racial stereotypes and prejudices, and casting Nuwaubian culture onto the global stage. Consequently, Nuwaubian literature emerged from this period with increased complexity, diversity, and recognition that continues to inform the genre to this day.

The latter half of the 20th and the dawning years of the 21st century bore witness to an evolved and intricate mosaic of Nuwaubian literature, meticulously chronicling the multifaceted panorama of the 'black' experience. Among the constellation of authors who have graced this era, moving luminaries such as Toni Morrison, Maya Angelou, and James Baldwin have emerged, capturing the adulation of critics and readers alike. Their riveting body of work underscores, with compelling resonance, the enduring pertinence and vigor of Nuwaubian literature, its capacity to serve as a reflective mirror illuminating the nation's convoluted historical labyrinth, and its innate drive to bear witness to the universal pursuit of freedom and dignity. The eloquent ink of these authors, ceaselessly flowing, continues to inscribe upon the pages of history the quintessential narratives that shape, define, and enhance the dialogue of the Nuwaubian journey.

Nuwaubian literature, thus, emerges as a rich symphony of voices, reverberating with the harmonies and dissonances of times past and present. A dynamic narrative, it ebbs and flows with the tides of history, constantly evolving yet always echoing the unrelenting song of the Nuwaubian experience - a song of resilience, of courage, of shared tribulation, and the relentless pursuit of freedom, justice, and identity in an ever-changing world.

Nuwaubian Hair

There is a long-standing debate in the Nuwaubian community about what, exactly, constitutes good hair. The root cause of this debate is deeply intertwined with our cultural history and racial discrimination. Nuwaubian hair can be characterized by its unique texture and styles. It is a symbol of Nuwaubian heritage and our African roots. For many Nuwaubians, it is not just hair, it is an emblem of our collective identity, historical resilience, societal dynamics, and serves as a testament to the Nuwaubian community's legacy of resistance and self-expression. The story of Nuwaubian hair predates our notion of civilization, it is truly a remarkable journey that channels millennia of cultural heritage.

Since our journey began in America, Nuwaubian hair has been subjected to Eurocentric standards of beauty and societal pressures to assimilate, leading to practices such as the forced shaving of enslaved individuals' heads during captivity. This dehumanizing act aimed to erase our cultural ties and strip away our identity, reflecting broader systemic racism. Even after emancipation, negative attitudes towards Afro-textured hair have persisted, perpetuated by discriminatory practices in schools and workplaces.

The natural hair movement emerged in response to these oppressive beauty standards, advocating for the celebration and acceptance of Nuwaubian hair in its natural state. Influenced by cultural figures and grassroots activism, this movement seeks to dismantle stereotypes and promote self-love among Nuwaubians. Legislation such as the CROWN Act represents a significant step towards combating hair-based discrimination, acknowledging the societal implications of racialized beauty standards. However, despite this progress, challenges persist, with instances of discrimination in schools, workplaces, and even within professional sports highlighting the ongoing struggle for social equality. Through advocacy, education, and cultural representation, the Nuwaubian community continues to reclaim its narrative surrounding hair, asserting pride and resilience in the face of adversity.

Nuwaubian Cuisine

Nuwaubian cuisine, often referred to as soul food, stands as a testament to the resilience and adaptability of a people who endured the horrors of slavery and ethnic oppression. Rooted in the American South, this culinary tradition emerged from the fusion of West African, Central African, Western European, and Indigenous American influences. Soul food finds its origins in the harsh realities of slavery, where enslaved Africans in the antebellum South were forced to make do with meager rations and undesirable scraps of food. Items like ham hocks, hog jowls, and pig intestines, rejected by white slave owners, became the building blocks of our cuisine. Enslaved Africans drew upon their culinary heritage, incorporating cooking techniques and ingredients from their native lands with the limited resources available to them.

Initially viewed as low-class fare, soul food evolved into a source of pride and cultural identity for millions of Nuwaubians, particularly during the mid-20th century amid the rise of the Black Power movement. Figures like LeRoi Jones (Amiri Baraka) and Elijah Muhammad played pivotal roles in shaping the narrative around soul food, with some, like Muhammad and Dick Gregory, criticizing its health implications while others embraced it as a symbol of resistance against cultural erasure.

The substantial African influence on soul food is evident in its use of spices, grains, and cooking techniques reminiscent of West and Central African culinary traditions. Staples like black-eyed peas, okra, and rice, as well as cooking methods such as open-pit roasting, reflect the richness of African gastronomy brought to the American South through the transatlantic slave trade. Native American culinary practices, particularly from southeastern tribes, also left an indelible mark on soul food. Corn, a staple of Indigenous diets, found its way into dishes like cornbread and grits, while techniques like nixtamalization influenced the preparation of maize-based foods. The interconnectedness of African and Native American cuisine underscores the complex history of the American South. European settlers in the South introduced livestock farming practices that shaped soul food, with dishes like chitlins (chitterlings) and liver mush, incorporating offal and organ meats common in European cuisines. This cultural exchange between enslaved Africans and European settlers further enriched the culinary landscape of the region.

While soul food continues to be celebrated for its rich flavors and cultural significance, concerns about its health implications persist. High in starch, fat, and sodium, traditional soul food dishes have been linked to health issues like hypertension and diabetes, prompting debates about how to preserve the authenticity of the cuisine while promoting healthier alternatives. Despite these challenges, soul food remains a cherished part of Nuwaubian heritage, deeply intertwined with social rituals and communal gatherings. From church picnics to holiday feasts, soul food continues to nourish both body and soul, serving as a reminder of the resilience and creativity of Nuwaubian people. Nuwaubian cuisine transcends its American origins to embody the enduring spirit of an African community that forged a distinctive culinary identity in the face of adversity. As soul food continues to evolve and adapt, it serves as a powerful symbol of cultural resilience and resistance against oppression.

Nuwaubian Names

'African American' names are deeply rooted in the history of Nuwaubian people, reflecting our struggle for identity and resistance against social and cultural oppression. Historically, African slaves were stripped of their names upon arrival to America, adopting names assigned by their white slaveholders. Before the mid-20th century, African American names closely mirrored those of European-Americans, with immigrants often changing their names to assimilate. However, distinctive Nuwaubian naming practices emerged as early as the Antebellum period, reflecting themes and patterns found in West African languages.

The Civil Rights Movement of the 1960s marked a turning point, leading to a dramatic rise in uniquely Nuwaubian or Afrocentric names. Influenced by the Black Power Movement and a growing emphasis on individuality, Nuwaubians began embracing names that celebrated their heritage. The Afrocentrism movement popularized African names and invented names imagined to be African sounding. Prefixes like La/Le and suffixes like -ique/-isha became common, along with inventive spellings and the use of punctuation marks. French, Muslim, and Biblical names also found their way into Nuwaubian culture, reflecting diverse influences and expressions of identity. However, workplace discrimination based on names remains a pervasive issue, with studies showing that applicants with traditionally "black or African" names face significant biases during employment screening processes.

In many cultures, especially African, names serve as more than just labels; they carry deep personal, cultural, familial, and historical meaning. In Ancient Khemet, naming was a profound rite that imparted a dual identity upon an individual. Each individual was bestowed with two names: a commonly used name for daily interactions, and a 'Ren,' or sacred spiritual name known to an intimate circle of family and the priest from which it was received. The Ren served a critical purpose beyond mortal existence. It was believed that the Ren held the key to maintaining a bond with the individual's soul in the afterlife, ensuring a connection that transcended the physical realm.

The practice of changing names among Nuwaubian continues to this day, often coinciding with significant life events such as religious conversions or involvement in movements promoting black empowerment. Figures like Muhammad Ali and Malcolm X famously changed their names to reflect their newfound identities and beliefs. Organizations like the Nation of Islam and The Nuwaubian Nation of Moors actively encourage Nuwaubians to abandon what they perceive as 'slave names' and adopt names of African origin, emphasizing the importance of reclaiming our cultural heritage and rejecting symbols of oppression. Despite ongoing challenges, Nuwaubians continue to assert their heritage and individuality through their names, resisting forced assimilation and reclaiming their identity in a society that often seeks to marginalize them.

10

What are Nuwaubian Languages?

anguage plays a crucial role in the culture, heritage, and comradery of a people. For Nuwaubians, our relationship with language is complex and multifaceted as a result of the historical context of slavery. Despite the claim that we "have no language of our own," it is important that we recognize how African American Vernacular English (AAVE), and unique cultural practices have contributed to a distinct linguistic identity. African American Vernacular English (AAVE), also known as Ebonics, is a dialect of English that is rooted in the "broken" speech of African slaves who were forced to abandon their native languages and communicate using English. AAVE has evolved over centuries, influenced by the linguistic practices of English, African, and other languages spoken by the European colonists and indigenous peoples of America. This evolution has resulted in a unique linguistic system with its own phonological, syntactic, and lexical rules, which serves as a marker of identity and solidarity within the Nuwaubian community.

AAVE allowed enslaved Africans and their descendants to maintain a sense of community and continuity with their African heritage and each other, despite brutal efforts to strip them of their culture. Moreover, the creative use of language in music and poetry showcases the rich linguistic and cultural innovation of the community. These artistic expressions have not only been a means of survival and resistance but have also influenced American culture and language at large. The claim that

"African Americans, have no language of their own" overlooks the profound contributions of our linguistic heritage which reflects the community's historical journey, creativity, and ongoing struggle for identity and recognition. Language, in this context, is not merely a means of communication but a testament to the 'black' experience, embodying the community's resilience, creativity, and enduring spirit.

The Creole Languages

Beyond our influence with African American Vernacular English, Nuwaubians have made substantial contributions to the development and proliferation of a multitude of argots, including creole languages. Creoles, characterized by their fusion and simplification of diverse linguistic elements, exhibit a remarkable tendency to organize inherited grammatical structures from parent languages while incorporating novel features. Unlike pidgins, which serve as simplified communication tools, creoles possess well-defined lexicons and grammatical systems, making them fully functional languages in their own right.

Historically, creole languages have emerged in regions deeply impacted by European colonialism, spanning the Americas, Africa, and Asia. Colonial expansion and trade facilitated the emergence of many creoles rooted in European languages such as English and French. While the lexicon of creole languages often reflects the influence of dominant social groups, their grammatical evolution follows distinct trajectories, yielding unique linguistic structures. Historically, creole languages have been stigmatized as inferior to their natal tongue. However, political and academic evolution has improved the status of creole languages, with some becoming official or semi-official languages.

Nuwaubians in North American, primarily associate the term "creole" with the French-based Louisiana Creole, known as Kouri-Vini. However, it is essential that we recognize the diverse manifestations of creole languages around the world. Examples include Ki-Nubi, a Sudanese-

Arabic based creole found in East Africa, Manglish the English based creole language spoken in Malaysia, and Kriol spoken in Australia. These varied expressions of creole languages underscore the rich linguistic heritage of not only Nuwaubians but people of color in general and their enduring impact on linguistic diversity across continents.

The Nuwaubic Languages

In 1989, As Sayyid Isa Al Haadi Al Mahdi, a prominent figure in the Ansaaru Allah Community and the founder of the Nuwaubian Nation of Moors, introduced "Nubic, The Language of the Nubian Americans." Nubic is a unique Sudanese lect (variety) of Arabic. Al Mahdi's decision to introduce Nubic to the Western Hemisphere was deliberate, stemming from its historical ties to the Nubians of antiquity. In choosing Nubic, Al Mahdi aimed to reconnect Nuwaubian people with the cultural and linguistic heritage of our Nubian ancestors, whose legacy endured through centuries of migration and displacement. Nubic, with its roots in ancient Nubian civilizations, symbolizes a link to the past and a means of cultural preservation in the contemporary context of the Western Hemisphere. Nubic represented a conscious effort to reclaim and revitalize a language that held deep significance for the Nuwaubian community, serving as a testament to the enduring legacy of Nubian culture in the diaspora.

In 1994, As Sayyid Isa Al Haadi Al Mahdi, as Nayya: Malachi Zodoq York-El, published The Teacher's Guide to the Nuwaubian Language. The Teacher's Guide to the Nuwaubian Language marked a significant milestone in the linguistic and cultural development of the Nuwaubian language. This comprehensive guide introduced the Rizqirian Script, and delineated what was then the three, now four, distinct Nuwaubian scripts. The Nubic script, introduced in 1989, based on a Sudanese lect of Arabic, mirroring its style, function, and offering a connection to the rich linguistic heritage of our Nubian ancestors. Nuwaubic, a pictorial language system reminiscent of ancient Khemetic or Nubian hieroglyphs, serves as a visual representation of Nuwaubian cultural motifs and concepts. Lastly, the Rizqirian script, also known as Nuwaubic, which is systematically akin to Western styles of writing with a lexicon rooted in Arabic and Hebrew. Since the publishing of the Teacher's Guide to the Nuwaubian Language in 1994, a new Nuwaubian script, 'Nuwaupic', has been introduced to the Western world. Nuwaupic utilizes a unique script composed of characters that closely resembles Sanskrit, the sacred language of classical Hindu philosophy.

The Nuwaubian languages are more than mere linguistic constructs; they represent a structured effort to establish a distinct cultural and linguistic framework within the Nuwaubian community. In developing and promoting these languages, the community asserts its self-determination and fosters a sense of unity and cohesion among Nuwaubian people. Moreover, the effort to develop and impart these languages underscores the significance of language in shaping and expressing communal and cultural identities. It reflects a deep-seated desire to reclaim and preserve our ethnic and cultural heritage, offering a means of communication that is exclusive to Nuwaubian people, and one that resonates with our historical, cultural, and spiritual lineage. In essence, the Nuwaubian languages are a pivotal step in the Nuwaubian journey toward establishing a distinct identity and social structure.

11

Politics & Religions

The late nineties and dawning of the new millennium marked a significant turning point for the Nuwaubian community with the emergence of what would eventually become known as the Conscious Community. Representing the next evolutionary phase of Nuwaubian identity and culture, the Conscious Community has been characterized as a loose network of individuals spanning the African Diaspora, united by a diverse range of Pan-African, Afrocentric, Afrofuturistic, Black Nationalist, and Black Liberationist ideologies, collectively termed as "black radical thought" by United States intelligence community. This collective consciousness within the community reflects a heightened awareness of social, political, and cultural issues impacting Nuwaubians at large.

Central to the ethos of the Conscious Community is the concept of being "conscious" or "woke," which goes beyond mere awareness to encompass a deep innerstanding of the interconnectedness of various dimensions of societal phenomena. This awareness encompasses cultural, ethical, historical, philosophical, and socioeconomic factors that shape the experiences of Nuwaubians and inform their collective struggle for freedom, recognition, and empowerment. Within this framework, being "woke" implies an active engagement with the complexities of contemporary issues and a commitment to addressing them from a nuanced and informed perspective.

The scope of the term "woke" broadened during the presidency of Barack Obama, particularly among conservative Republicans who used it as a pejorative to dismiss progressive ideologies associated with identity politics and social justice. However, its original context implies the markings of acute social awareness and an enthusiastic commitment to advancing the interests and aspirations of Nuwaubians and throughout the diaspora.

My introduction to "Conscious Community" occurred shortly after the tragic loss of a close friend. Prior to this unfortunate incident, my encounters with the various forms of "right knowledge" (e.g., Holy Tabernacle Ministries, Nation of Islam, Moorish Science Temple, various writing from a diversity of authors on different subjects relating to history, struggle, and future of "Black" people) were, for the most part, in isolation. I can recall only having one close friend with whom I could discuss these new revelations. After engaging in several months of heated debate, he began to acknowledge the validity of this new thought process that resulted from my introduction to Right Knowledge.

Growing up in a small Bible-belt city, known only for its gang culture, my exposure to diversity of conscious thought within the Nuwaubian community was extremely limited. However, upon moving to the Atlanta Metropolitan Area, I found myself immersed in a diverse environment of personalities and ideologies from across the broader spectrum of conscious people. My nascent knowledge of self and hip-hop aspiration kept me closely tethered to various facets of the conscious community.

Social Media & The Conscious Community

The proliferation of social media dramatically expanded the reach of the conscious community, leveraging interactive technologies and online platforms to foster the creation, distribution, consumption of Pan-African, Afrocentric, and Black Nationalist content and merchandise.

Platforms like Blog Talk Radio paved the way for internet radio shows such as Culture Freedom Radio, hosted by Sun Re 9, and the African History hosted by Michael Imhotep. Video blogging and sharing platforms, like YouTube, became a dais for emerging intellectuals, teachers, leaders, separatists, subverters, and militants, with channels like Sa Neter TV. Even Roland Martin, the former executive editor of the Chicago Defender, author, and TV personality, utilizes social media to shed light on issues pertinent to the Nuwaubian people, boldly addressing racial injustice, and fervently advocating for political engagement within the Nuwaubian community.

Social media platforms have enabled members of the conscious community to share knowledge, historical insights, and cultural achievements that are often overlooked or underrepresented in mainstream educational systems. Access to this information has empowered individuals with a deeper understanding of their heritage, fostering a sense of pride and identity. Social media has also proven a powerful tool for activism within the Nuwaubian community. It has facilitated the organization of protests, conveyed evidence of social injustice, and mobilized community members on a global scale. The Black Lives Matter movement, for example, gained international attention largely through social media, highlighting issues of police brutality and racial inequality.

While social media has many positive aspects, it has also presented significant challenges. The spread of misinformation can be particularly damaging, leading to divisions within the community and undermining the credibility of legitimate individuals and organizations. Social media platforms have been used to perpetuate stereotypes, promote racism, and provide safe harbor for the harassment of people across all ethnicities. Studies have shown that constant exposure to instances of racial injustice, discrimination, and violence on social media can lead to increased feelings of depression, anxiety, and stress, particularly when users are regularly confronted with traumatic content.

The monetization of social media content introduced the dynamic of profit motivation, ultimately transforming the landscape of conscious engagement. Initially driven by a genuine desire to disseminate awareness and education, this noble endeavor gradually transformed into a lucrative for-profit venture. This shift preceded a broader trend, where the cultivation and sharing of content within the broader Nuwaubian community burgeoned into a colossal domestic industry, now valued at approximately twenty-four billion dollars. As the potential for revenue and notoriety blossomed, what were once grassroots street corner ciphers, had been supplanted by more sophisticated and commercially viable mediums. Debates and discussions transitioned to live video-streamed events, promoted across various media platforms, and staged in front of large fervid audiences. These debate battles, as they were called, not only provide a platform for sharing ideas but also became spectacles of entertainment and sources of revenue.

This pivot towards profit fundamentally altered the dynamics within conscious communities. While it undoubtedly increased visibility and allowed for broader dissemination of ideas, it also introduced new challenges. The lure of profit, coupled with the desire for fame, exacerbated the already contentious nature of discussions around politics and religion. Such topics, inherently divisive, became all the more charged in an environment where the stakes were not just ideological but financial as well. In this monetized setting, the original intent of spreading knowledge and fostering community solidarity took a backseat to the objectives of engagement, viewership, and revenue generation. Conflicts, once perhaps engaged in solely for the sake of truth and enlightenment, now had the added dimensions of competing for audience attention and financial gain. This transformation illustrates a broader societal trend where monetization can significantly impact the nature and outcomes of cultural and intellectual exchanges, making the environment ripe for conflict not only because of differing ideologies but also due to the underlying motives of profit and notoriety.

Woke

In 2017, I made the personal decision to take a step back from the Conscious Community. I had become jaded with the behavior of community members. In addition to profit motivation, an unhealthy focus on notoriety and the mis-overstanding of religion had debauched the integrity of the community. I watch community members become increasingly arrogant. I witnessed individuals and groups established on freedom and equality for Nuwaubian people shift toward Black Racial Supremacy. Black men and women were unduly indulging the idea that the "Black" man and woman were the god and goddesses of the universe while simultaneously presuming that all white men and women were devils. Not because all white men and women had individually committed some act of evil beyond that of the average human turpitude. But, simply because of their white skin. This same type of subjective thinking deceived millions of Europeans into thinking they were impune to their acts of inhumanity and crimes against the human family. They now bare the shame of these acts committed by their predecessors.

The notion of mankind's interconnectedness with the divine architect of the universe is nothing new. As far as human history is concerned, this concept originated millennia ago in the earliest of Nile River Valley civilizations. This idea is encapsulated in the maxim "Man know thyself, and ye shall know the Universe and the Gods" which has been inscribed in various ancient lodges around the world. It suggests a profound overstanding of the unity between individuals and the cosmos. This overstanding predates and informs many contemporary religious and philosophical teachings, such as John 10:30-38 in which Isho/Yeshua alludes to this principle when he suggests that "I and the father are one." Mankind is but a manifestation of the Almighty.

However, mankind is not the only manifestation of the Almighty. This unity extends beyond humanity to encompass all of existence. Every sentient being, every living entity, and even the inanimate objects that fill the cosmos are expressions of Universal Intelligence, Universal Life Force, and Universal Objectivity (body). All of which are the result of a purposeful and deliberate act of creation. It challenges us to see beyond superficial differences and recognize the divine spark within all forms of life, promoting a worldview that values inclusiveness, respect, and compassion over divisiveness.

The notion that anyone could perceive themselves as divinely superior, the Almighty Maker, Creator, and Sustainer of the Universe, while simultaneously allowing themselves to be robbed of everything, up to and including their own identity (knowledge of self) reflects a paradox deeply rooted in the trauma and dissonance of Nuwaubian people. This cognitive dissonance results when individuals are stripped of their heritage, identity, and basic human dignity through the selfish evils of slavery, colonization, and systemic oppression. In essence, it is but a desperate attempt to reclaim some sort of dignity and assert autonomy through inherent divinity and superiority. However, such assertions contrast starkly with their lived realities of systemic dependency and the lingering shadows of historical subjugation that continue to influence the socio-economic landscape of their descendants.

The historical context of slavery and the oppression of our Nubian ancestors is not just a story of physical bondage. It is the story of the systematic erasure of our cultural, spiritual, and intellectual heritage. It is a story of deliberate acts of violence, aimed at not just controlling the physical bodies of enslaved individuals but to obliterate their connection to their past, their knowledge of self, and their understanding of their place in the world. The brutality inflicted upon them—ranging from physical torture and sexual violence to psychological warfare and cultural genocide—was a multifaceted assault on their posterity. Yet, a midst this darkness, the resilience and perseverance exhibited by our ancestors has been monumental, a testament to the indomitable spirit of survival and resistance against dehumanization.

The assertion of superiority based on race, divine inheritance, or other criteria over others within the human family raises a serious moral and ethical question. It poses a direct contradiction to the fundamental principles of equality, interconnectedness, and mutual respect that are the foundation to every benevolent moral and spiritual system across the planet. Whether we choose to accept it or not, most Nuwaubians are completely dependent on this system. Regardless of whether you are self-employed or unemployed, rich or poor, a doctor or high school dropout, woke or eyes-wide shut, until you, your family, and your wealth are outside of the geopolitical borders of the United States of America your existence, subsistence, and livelihood is inextricably tied to the fate of this country. While striving for self-determination and independence is a noble and critical pursuit, the reality of globalization, world-wide economic interdependence, and the lingering effects of imperialism make complete extrication nearly impossible. The journey towards genuine autonomy and self-realization necessitates a collective effort to dismantle oppressive structures, establish equitable systems of governance, and foster a global community rooted in mutual respect, tolerance, and a shared responsibility for the planet's wellbeing.

12 |

Conspiracy Theories

Narratives surrounding the U.S. black elite can be traced back to the era before the Civil War, particularly among free "Black" people who acquired property. The "black elite" played a significant role in abolition, the Underground Railroad, and pioneered various professions during the Reconstruction Era. The emergence of prominent figures like James Beckwourth, Langston Hughes, Arthur Ashe, Barack Obama, and Kamala Harris emphasizes the diverse contributions of Nuwaubians across various spheres of American life. The historical contributions of black elites to American society, culture, and politics are a complex story of the meshing of ethnicity, identity, and class. The evolution of the black elite class over time, from historical figures who challenged slavery and colonialism to contemporary professionals and politicians, accentuates the dynamic nature of Nuwaubian leadership and influence in America and around the globe. Sigma Pi Phi and The Links, Inc., are two predominantly Nuwaubian organizations that were founded as spaces for professional Nuwaubian men and affluent Nuwaubian women. Sigma Pi Phi became a haven for Nuwaubian men excluded from mainstream professional circles, while The Links, Inc., formed in 1946, provided a platform for Nuwaubian women to engage in social and intellectual activities. Members of these organizations have been at the forefront of significant social changes, including civil rights advocacy and philanthropy, emphasizing education, health, and the arts.

Sigma Pi Phi, also known as The Boulé (the ancient Greek word for "The Council"), serves as the oldest Nuwaubian fraternity created in America. Unlike traditional college fraternities, Sigma Pi Phi caters to professional gentlemen beyond their collegiate years and who are well established in their careers. Founded on May 15, 1904, in Philadelphia, Pennsylvania, the fraternity was born out of necessity for Nuwaubian professionals who were excluded from the professional and cultural associations of the "white" community at the time. It boasts over 5,000 members across 139 chapters globally, including in the United States, the United Kingdom, The Bahamas, Colombia, and Brazil. The founders of Sigma Pi Phi were distinguished in their fields, comprising two doctors, a dentist, and a pharmacist, who sought to create a space for intellectual and social engagement among professional Nuwaubian men. Membership to Sigma Pi Phi is known for its exclusivity and has historically included members from other Black Greek-letter organizations, highlighting a network of cross-membership among Nuwaubian fraternities. Notable members of Sigma Pi Phi include historic civil rights leaders such as W.E.B. Du Bois, Dr. Martin Luther King Jr., and Robert J. Abele (also members of Alpha Phi Alpha Fraternity, Inc.,), NAACP leader Kweisi Mfume (also a member of Omega Psi Phi Fraternity, Inc.), Nobel Peace Prize winner Ralph Bunche (Alpha Phi Alpha Fraternity, Inc.), political leaders such as Maynard Jackson (Alpha Phi Alpha Fraternity, Inc.) and Douglas Wilder (Omega Psi Phi Fraternity, Inc.), and business leaders like Kenneth Chenault (also a member of Phi Beta Sigma Fraternity, Inc.) of American Express. The fraternity's reach extends to various sectors, reflecting its influence across civil rights, politics, academia, and business.

The Links, Inc., headquartered in Washington, D.C., is a prestigious invitation-only social and service organization for prominent Nuwaubian women. The Links was formed in 1946 by seven affluent women, all married to influential men, who sought to create a platform for social and intellectual engagement among Nuwaubian women. Over the years, the organization transitioned from a group of opulent wives to a powerhouse of women, boasting 16,000 members across nearly three hundred chapters, who have become influential in their own right. This shift led to a change in internal dynamics, reflecting a generational evolution of leadership within the organization. Like, Sigma Pi Phi, membership in The Links is highly exclusive, requiring nomination by a current member and often favoring candidates known to a sizable portion of the chapter's membership. The organization's exclusivity has faced criticism, but it remains a marker of social, professional, and economic prominence within the Nuwaubian community.

Links members are required to commit to voluminous volunteer hours, raising funds for various causes including education, health, and the arts. Their social events serve as significant gatherings for the "black" elite, emphasizing their role in promoting philanthropy and community service. Among its distinguished members are the likes of Kamala Harris (also a member Alpha Kappa Alpha Sorority, Inc.), Marian Wright Edelman (Delta Sigma Theta Sorority, Inc.), and the late Dr. Betty Shabazz (wife of slain civil rights leader El Hajj Malik El Shabazz also known as Malcom X, and member of Delta Sigma Theta Sorority, Inc.). Other prominent members include politicians like Joyce Beatty (Delta Sigma Theta Sorority, Inc.), Keisha Lance Bottoms (Delta Sigma Theta Sorority Inc.), Val Demings (Delta Sigma Theta Sorority, Inc.), Sheila Jackson Lee (Alpha Kappa Alpha Sorority, Inc.), Ayanna Pressley (Delta Sigma Theta Sorority, Inc.), and Frederica Wilson (Alpha Kappa Alpha Sorority, Inc.); among other civil rights leaders and activists; as well as judges, doctors, bankers, and educators. These women exemplify the organization's influence across various sectors, contributing significantly to their communities and beyond.

Despite their continuous commitment to leaderships, service, and community advancement exclusive organization such as Sigma Pi Phi, The Links, Inc., Black Greek Letter Organizations, and various masonic organizations have been the subject of speculation, particularly in the conscious community. Conspiracy theories regarding these organizations suggest hidden agendas and maintenance of the status quo, portraying them as shadowy influencers within the Nuwaubian community. These narratives, often speculative and lacking empirical evidence, raise valid questions as to the dynamics of class, power, and representation within the Nuwaubian community. Nevertheless, prominent African American men and women within these organizations have played pivotal roles in civil rights and politics. Figures like the late congressman John Lewis of Phi Beta Sigma, demonstrate the interconnectedness of these organizations within the broader civil rights movements. Women of The Links, such as congresswomen Sheila Jackson Lee, exemplify the organization's influence in politics and advocacy, showing the evolving nature of the "black" elite from supporting roles to centers of influence. The history and evolution of the so-called "black" elite in America, marked by organizations like Sigma Pi Phi and The Links, showcases the profound contributions of Nuwaubians to societal progress. Through leadership, philanthropy, and advocacy, these groups and their members embody the diversity and dynamism of "black" excellence, challenging narratives of exclusivity with their impactful work in communities across the nation and the world.

Conspiracy Theories

The reverse side of the U.S. One Dollar Bill features the Great Seal of the United States, often mistaken for a Masonic emblem. Albeit the seal does incorporate many masonic elements. The Latin inscription "Annuit Coeptis", whose literal translation is "He nodded to the people" is situated above the masonic "eye of providence", not to be mistaken for the Eye of Horus. Together, they imply that a provident "or prudent" watcher (i.e., God) nodded in affirmation to the people. The "Eye of Providence" suspended above an unfinished pyramid consisting of thirteen steps, represents the thirteen original American colonies that are the foundation of a then unfinished nation. Novus Ordo Seclorum, which literally translate to "New Order of the Ages" refers to what they incorrectly believed to be the first democracy on the planet earth. The Roman numerical inscription at the base of the pyramid equates to 1776, the year in which the United States of America was founded and proclaimed its independence from the British Crown.

The Great Seal of the United States has long been the subject of conspiracy theories and speculations. During the spring of 2023, I can recall receiving a Facebook notification about a trending post in an African history group of which I am a member. The post contained a photo that closely resembled the Great Seal of the United States. However, the Roman numerical inscription at the base of the pyramid had been altered to reflect a date other than 1776. The author of the post simply asked that the audience explain the meaning. Although the post had been trending, achieving hundreds of responses in less than an hour, only one person prior to myself pointed out that the Roman numerical inscription had been altered. As is usually the case, members of the groups responded with a range of conspiracy theories targeted at secret societies such as the Illuminati, covert government entities such as the New World Order, and cults with secret esoteric agendas. None of which were based on substantive facts or evidence outside of your top selling amazon conspiracy theory genre.

As I set out about my normal course of action of trying to dispel misinformation and further rational thought, I received a peculiar reaction to one of my replies to another Facebook user from whom I assume was a mixed-race or extremely fair skinned Israelite of the Rastafarian school of thought. He simply stated, "I will never follow you!" to which I replied with an "Okay" and thumbs up. Apparently, I irritated this gentleman by challenging the validity of the evidence on which he chose to base his argument to equate the Great Seal of the United States with a cryptic Illuminati symbol representing a one world government. For years I had felt that there were Nuwaubian intentionally spreading misinformation for whatever reasons. However, it was at this moment that

I realized the pervasiveness of misinformation was not that simple. Not that I had been looking for followers, but I had been looking for a group of intelligent, highly resolute, and motivated Nuwaubians from various cultural and religious backgrounds with whom I could build. It was through this brother's comment that I realized that I could never truly advance any further than my ethnic identity and culture would allow. Even Sean "Jay-Z" Carter, in all his wealth, stills identifies and is identified by others as a "black" man in America. This is not to say that he, or anyone else for that matter, would allow their ethnic identity and culture to hold them back. It is just to say that irrespective of how intelligent, wealthy, or special we might feel we are, we can never truly rise above the groups with which we are identified.

The danger in conspiracy theories is not such much that they are normally lies that diminish the reputations of philanthropic organizations, it is the dissemination of misinformation, erosion of trust, and potential for hyper-polarization that works to undermine the laudable undertakings of good men and women. Intentionally, or even unwittingly, spreading misinformation can have serious and sometimes fatal consequences, especially in the current political climate of the United States. Misinformation about the 2020 US Presidential Election being "stolen" fueled the January 6th storming of the United States Capital, resulting in death, injury, and lingering political and racial enmity. A particular subset of American have a long history of using misinformation to incite ethnic or religious violence, especially against communities of color. In perpetuating unsubstantiated theories about secret alliances with white supremacist organizations and hidden agendas to maintain the status quo we negate more than a century of progress toward true freedom, justice, and equality. We erode trust in the few institutions that we do have outside of the sanctioned "black church", many of which (especially Black Greek Letter Organizations) were founded during the era of Jim Crow, a time during which Nuwaubian men, women, and children were being lynched with impunity. Between 1900 and 1910, the decade during which Sigma Pi Phi, Alpha Phi Alpha Fraternity, Inc., and Alpha Kappa Alpha Sorority, Inc., were established there were a total of 858 documented lynchings (Archives at Tuskegee Institute. n.d.). The men and women who founded these organizations were the revolutionary heroes of their day.

To combat the pervasiveness of conspiracy theories in the Nuwaubian Community, it is critical that educational and public institutions promote media literacy and critical thinking skills among Nuwaubian youth. We must provide accessible resources that explain the historical context and symbolism of these individuals and organizations to help counteract misinformation. Encouraging open and informed discussions about the difference between legitimate historical inquiry and unfounded conspiracy theories is also vital in preserving the mental and psychological health of the Nuwaubian community. Digital conspiracy theories represent a significant and growing threat in the Age of the Internet. Misinformation tends to spread rapidly through social media platforms, and other online channels, reaching vast audiences with unprecedented speed. These theories often exploit fears, uncertainties, and the human tendency to seek patterns (inferences), even where none exist. Efforts to combat digital conspiracy theories include fact-checking initiatives, media literacy education, and the implementation of content moderation. However, these approaches face challenges, including balancing censorship and freedom of expression, the effectiveness of fact-checking, changing deeply held beliefs, and the global scale of digital misinformation.

13

The Great American Narrative

Mainstream society has a history of demonizing anything that does not further what I call the "Great American Narrative". The Great American Narrative is the highly subjective and predominantly white view of America's past greatness. This narrative is reflected in the "Make America Great Again" or MAGA (which ironically is the Latin word for witch) movement and is based mostly on the perspective of a certain group of "white" Americans. The comfort and luxury experienced by the mostly white ruling class during times of supposed prosperity are simultaneously perceived as living nightmares for many communities of color.

During the Black Power movement, mainstream media often depicted the Black Panther Party as armed militants seeking to disrupt society and overthrow the government. However, this portrayal overlooks the party's significant contributions, such as the establishment of free nutrition programs and free healthcare clinics. The Black Panther Party for Self Defense was organized around the purpose of protecting black communities from police brutality, a reality that was denied by mainstream society until the infamous beating of Rodney King on March 3, 1991. With the advent of modern telecommunications and social media, the world has become increasingly aware of the frequency and severity of police brutality in black communities. The reality of police brutality in communities of color serves as a constant threat to the Great American Narrative.

Simultaneously, white America has attempted to portray figures like George Washington, Thomas Jefferson, Andrew Jackson, Martin Van Buren, William Henry Harrison, Ulysses S. Grant, and other American presidents as great heroes. These figures are celebrated despite their involvement with slavery and the oppression of Nuwaubian people. While some, like George Washington and Ulysses S. Grant, eventually emancipated their slaves, their actions do not erase the history of exploitation and cruelty. To his credit President Ulysses S. Grant freed the one slave he was given by his father-in-law shortly after receiving title (of the property not the Title of President). Despite these actions, the legacy of slavery and systemic racism continues to shape American society, challenging the notion of heroism associated with these figures and highlighting the ongoing struggle for "racial" equality.

I am not advocating for the erasure of these figures from American history. In spite of his history with slavery I admire General George Washington, who on his death bed declared the emancipation of his slaves upon the passing of his wife. However, I do feel that we as Americans should reevaluate the qualities that constitute heroism. Heroism is not necessarily exclusive to moral perfection, nor does it readily append itself to moral turpitude. In reality, many of our heroes are flawed individuals that apotheosize to divine majesty in the moment. In our minds, they live frozen in this moment, until some revelation awakens us to their imperfection. It is important that future generations of American citizens overstand the unadulterated truth of American history, imperfections, and all.

Emulating Leadership

As children we naturally aspire to emulate our heroes. These aspirations do not bequeath us in adulthood, if anything, they increase in intricacy and detail. Having grown up in a single-parent household, absent of a male role model, my initial notion of male heroism was rooted in the fictional super-heroes that I watched on television. As I grew older, my notion of heroism evolved to reflect my evolving interactions in American society. During my preadolescent and adolescent years my interactions were influenced by a different set of social elements. My heroes reflected an adolescent's immature concept of what it meant to prevail against the adversities associated with inner-city youths.

This immature concept of heroism accompanied me until I was fortunate enough to encounter Nuwaubu at the age of eighteen, at which time my concept of heroism evolved. That is not to say that all of my preadolescent and adolescent heroes were deleterious. As previously stated, our heroes are often flawed individuals that apotheosize to near divine majesty in the moment. During my teenage years, my list of heroes was extensive and like most children in my community it included the likes of Martin Luther King, Jr., Malcom X, Tupac Shakur, Nas, Outkast, Michael Jordon, and a slew of others. When I encountered Nuwaubu, my heroes evolved to include the likes of Afeni and Mutula Shakur, Huey P. Newton, Bobby Seal, Stockley Carmichael, Minister Louis Farrakhan, Malachi Z. York, and a lot more.

Emulation is not merely about imitating someone's actions; rather, it involves aspiring to match or surpass the achievements of our heroes. Through my personal journey, I have encountered numerous leaders across various organizations and institutions. However, within the Conscious and broader Nuwaubian community, leadership often appears to be limited in type and style. By leadership "style", I mean the methods, characteristics, and behaviors used in guiding, motivating, or managing others. Leadership style is normally influenced by past experiences (good and bad), personality, values, and skills. It is understandable why certain leaders thrive while others falter, as they must adapt to the evolving needs of an organization. What works during periods of stability or growth may not necessarily be effective during periods of turmoil and uncertainty. Therefore, flexibility and adaptability are crucial qualities for effective leadership in any environment.

14

A Legacy of Sorts

During the 18th century, most white Protestants denied the souls and humanity of African people, which excluded them from many Christian faith communities. However, as attitudes shifted, white Christians, recognizing slavery as a means of forced conversation, began efforts to convert enslaved Africans to Christianity. This practice was met with resistance from slave owners who feared potential revolts, a mindset that reinforced the brutality of slavery. Nevertheless, enslaved individuals found ways to practice their beliefs in secret, resisting oppression through covert religious gatherings.

Before the Civil War, Christianity was often introduced to slave populations by slave owners or revivalists. Southern whites contended that Christianity and slavery were compatible, exploiting biblical references to justify their position and advocating for a paternalistic approach. This theocratic authoritarian ideology, deeply ingrained in the Antebellum South, supported the institution of slavery, and perpetuated its systemic oppression. Despite the oppression and control imposed by slave owners, enslaved individuals gathered in "Hush Harbors" or invisible churches to practice their faith. These meetings were held under the cover of darkness to avoid detection. Hush Harbors and invisible churches provided a sanctuary for enslaved Africans to blend African religious traditions with Christianity, often expressing themselves through song and dance. Negro spirituals were born out of hush harbors! However, participation in these gatherings carried the risk of severe punishment if discovered by slave owners or overseers, highlighting the subversive nature of their religious practices.

Invisible churches emerged as informal Christian groups within the enslaved populations, offering a congenial alternative to the messaging at white-controlled churches. Congregants chose their own preachers who emphasized spiritual autonomy and resistance to slave masters' authority, providing a source of comfort and empowerment for some slaves. However, others faced difficulties accessing or aligning with these teachings. On larger plantations were slave owners promoted Christianity, "praise houses" or "prayer houses" were erected as simple structures within the plantation complex designed for use by enslaved people. These spaces served as early iterations of the "black" church, fostering Christian practice and community among the enslaved. Despite being controlled by slave masters, praise houses provided a venue for prayer, song, and religious expression, often mirroring the spontaneous nature of slave religion. After the American Civil War, some of these invisible churches evolved into organized black churches, such as the Black Episcopal Church, marking a significant transition in the history of black Christianity in America.

The Moorish Divine Movement

Post slavery or "Off the plantation" our history with Theocratic Authoritarianism can be traced as far back as Noble Drew Ali. Born Timothy Drew, Noble Drew Ali is the founder of the Moorish Science Temple of America. Little is known about Ali prior to his founding of the Canaanite Temple in 1913. Ali built the Canaanite Temple, The Moorish Divine National Movement, and Moorish Temple of Science, collectively the Moorish Science Temple of America, upon the premise that black people here in the Americas are descendants of Moabites and thus are "Moorish" by nationality, and Islamic by faith. Noble Drew Ali advocated that "black" people return to Islam and encouraged use of the term

"Moor" rather than black in self-identification. Rigorous obedience to the Prophet's regulations were required, and certain foods were forbidden.

During Ali's travels in Egypt, he reportedly encountered an Egyptian Magi who considered him a reincarnation of various religious prophets. It is said that this Magi trained Ali in Egyptian mysticism, the "Mysteries," and gave him a "lost section" of the Quran which is known today as the Circle Seven Koran or the Holy Koran of the Moorish Science Temple of America. The Circle 7 Koran and Islam, as it is practiced by "Moors" of the Moorish Science Temple, is altogether a distinct from the Quran and Islam, as it is practiced by two billion Muslims around the world.

The first nineteen chapters of the Circle 7 Koran were supposedly taken from Levi H. Dowling's 'The Aquarian Gospel of Jesus the Christ'. Even if not directly plagiarized, it is likely derived from the same source, which Dowling suggest as the 'Akashic' records[1]. At least fifteen chapters of the Circle 7 Koran are taken whole, or in part, from the Rosicrucian work 'Unto Thee I Grant' a popular read among Fraters and Soros around the world. Regardless, to suggest that Ali's intentions were malevolent would be a vast overstatement. Having emerged less than half a century after 246 years of slavery, Ali founded the first officially state-registered Islamic organization in America. Ali is also credited with being the first American born Islamic leader. To his devotees and supporters Noble Drew Ali is rightfully a savior and a Prophet. One such devotee, Wallace D. Fard also known as Wali Fard Muhammad, would go on to found the Nation of Islam.

The Nation of Yahweh

Founded in 1979 by Hulon Mitchel, Jr., also known as Yahweh ben Yahweh, the Nation of Yahweh emerged as a predominantly Black Hebrew Israelite religious movement in Miami, FL. Yahweh is one of the proper names of the Abrahamic deity of the Bible and the Torah. Yahweh ben Yahweh implies "God, the son of God." This unique identification sets the Nation of Yahweh apart from other Black Hebrew Israelite groups, cementing Yahweh ben Yahweh's vital role as the "Son of God" within the movement.

Mitchell's leadership over his followers was characterized by an authoritarian control that permeated every aspect of their lives. Dictating their clothing choices, regulating their eating habits, and even exercising control over their sex lives. It has been said by some that he wielded dominance over the most intimate facets of their existence. His influence extended beyond mere directives; he maintained intimate relationships with many female followers, blurring the lines between spiritual guidance and personal entanglements. In a candid admission to the New York Times, he rejected celibacy within the group, affirming his authority over the sexual behavior of his adherents.

[1] The Akashic records are believed by theosophists to be encoded in the mental plane. There is no scientific evidence to suggest the existence of such records.

15 |

Nuwaubian Nation of Moors

The story of Malachi Z. York's life and contributions form a complex and multifaceted journey, interwoven with a broad array of philosophical, spiritual, religious, and occult teachings. However, York's life and legacy are also marred by controversy and scandal, including legal troubles that have led to significant debate and division among his followers and observers. Despite these challenges, his work has left a lasting impact on many, with his writings and teachings continuing to be studied and followed by those who align with his vision for spiritual enlightenment and cultural revival. Under his leadership, the Ansaaru Allah Community, and other groups founded by York have pursued various educational, economic, and social initiatives aimed at improving the conditions and well-being of Nuwaubian people. His teachings encouraged self-awareness, community solidarity, and a return to what he viewed as authentic spiritual and cultural practices.

York's early life is shrouded in mystery! Differing stories about his upbringing have led to some confusion and differing accounts of his origins. According to the United States government Malachi Z. York was born on June 26th, 1945, as Dwight D. York of Boston, MA. Likewise, it has also been suggested that York, also known as As Sayyid Isa Al Haadi Al Mahdi, is of Nubian descent and has connections to Sudan and Sufi Islam through his farther Sayyid Hadi Abdulrahman Al Mahdi, to which York himself has previously alluded. He is also said to have originated from Ghana, New York, New Jersey, and Maryland.

It is also worth noting As Sayyid Isa Al Haadi Al Mahdi's uncanny ability to fluently speak multiple languages including various Arabic dialects, Hebrew, Aramaic, Coptic, Ge'ez, Latin, and English. It has been suggested that Al Mahdi's insight into language, religious texts, and ancient wisdom is divinely ordained. His remarkable linguistic ability served not only to elevate his status among his adherents but also to authenticate the eclectic teachings he promulgated through the Ansaaru Allah Community and its bookstore known as the Tents of Kedar. Al Mahdi himself has avowed his fluency in multiple languages as part of his spiritual and scholarly persona, suggesting that his linguistic skills were both a testament to his extensive self-education and divine guidance. Al Mahdi's teachings often incorporated elements from various languages, scripts, and cultures, cementing his image as a knowledgeable and divinely inspired leader.

As Sayyid Isa Al Haadi Al Mahdi founded the Ansaaru Allah Community (AAC) in Brooklyn, New York, during the early seventies. The AAC was part of Al Mahdi's broader mission to broaden the overstanding of Islam, Christianity, Judaism, and "occult " religions within Nuwaubian communities while uplifting the people and reconnecting them with what he described as their rightful spiritual and cultural heritages. The AAC aligned itself with African culture and heritage, emphasizing connections to ancient civilizations of the African continent. AL Mahdi's teachings often reflected a narrative that sought to reconnect Nuwaubian people with their various spiritually rich African backgrounds and traditions. During its peak, the Ansaaru Allah Community was known to have attracted a significant following within urban centers, particularly among blacks seeking spiritual alternatives that offered a sense of connectedness to African heritage and identity. The AAC's activities, including religious services, educational programs, and business enterprises reflect its substantial base of participants and supporters. However, the extent to which Al Mahdi and the Ansaaru Allah

Community had tangible ties to Sudan or Africa is not well documented and evidence of formal or practical ties is not widely available.

Holy Tabernacle Ministries

Throughout the years York's organizations have undergone a series of evolutions, name changes, and shifts in direction. As with other aspects of his teachings, Holy Tabernacle Ministries (HTM), a scion of the Tents of Kedar, generated a mixture of admiration, controversy, and criticism. Malachi Z. York founded HTM as part of his evolving religious and spiritual mission. HTM simultaneously operated as a community outreach and bookstore, disseminating the teachings of Malachi Z. York which included reinterpretations of various religious text, explanations of ancient mysteries, and detailed "narratives" about the influence of extraterrestrials on human affairs and spirituality. Holy Tabernacle Ministries was a self-publishing powerhouse, serving as a key avenue for the production and distribution of numerous books, pamphlets, scrolls, and other written materials.

One of the most distinctive characteristics of Holy Tabernacle Ministries was the introduction of advanced, sometimes controversial, ideas which York presented as revelations intended to enlighten Nuwaubian people about their origins and place in the world. "The Ministry" positioned itself as a hub for the distribution of divine knowledge. However, its operations transcended traditional doctrinal instruction, encompassing educational and social programs such as its prison outreach program. These efforts were part of a broader strategy to establish a self-sufficient, enlightened community that lived in accordance with ancient African principles and wisdom. HTM's reach extended internationally as well, with branches and affiliations across the United States, England, Canada, Trinidad, and Jamaica, serving as a testament to the compelling nature of York's literary works and indicative of The Ministry's successful business model.

The Ministry's literary corpus is characterized by its diversity and depth. The proliferation of these materials contributed to HTM's financial success, as the sale of these literary works helped to fund community initiatives. HTM thus became a self-sustaining entity within a network of organizations, contributing significantly to the financial growth of the Nuwaubian community. Through its global distribution of literature and the establishment of community centers, HTM achieved significant presence and commercial viability, with gross sales that underscore its role as a cornerstone in the Nuwaubian empire.

Holy Tabernacle Ministries, under the aegis of Malachi Z. York, represents a significant chapter in the dynamic and evolutionary narrative of his religious and spiritual teachings. HTM emerged as a beacon of a widening cultural movement. The Ministry's ability to maintain a consistent revenue stream through its various ventures demonstrates economic sustainability and strategic agility in market engagement. Holy Tabernacle Ministries was not merely a religious congregation but a conglomerate of diversified ventures spanning across continents. It was the embodiment of how religious movements can intersect with enterprising business strategies to create sustainability and globalization.

The Nuwaubian Nation of Moors

The Nuwaubian Nation of Moors, as a distinct entity, emerged in the 1990s. However, its origins can be traced back to the 1970s with the Ansaaru Allah Community. The diverse spiritual practices and beliefs of the Nuwaubian Nation of Moors reflected the diversity of the Nuwaubian people drawing from various "African" theologies, Black Liberation, Black Nationalism, and Afrocentric world history. Central to each of these beliefs was the importance of Nuwaubian people rediscovering and reconnecting with their "African" heritage. York's spiritual teachings included a synthesis of spiritual, mystical, and esoteric knowledge, suggesting insights into the true nature of the universe, human history, and metaphysical reality. These teachings included the ancient idea of intelligent life throughout the physical universe.

Malachi Z. York always firmly held that "Nuwaubu is not a religion." As articulated by York, "Nuwaubu is the Science of Sound Right Reason!". Nuwaubu is also a language. Specifically, Nuwaubu is a language composed of either the Nuwaubian or Rizqirian script. Nuwaubu is also a culture, the culture of Nuwaubian people. Nuwaubian 'culture' is reflective of its emphasis on Afrocentricity, as "African" people and their descendants possess a glorious heritage, notably tracing our lineage back to the earliest Nile River Valley civilizations. York, like others before him, advocated for self-identification and the pursuit of autonomy, emphasizing a unique ethnic identity distinct from mainstream American categories such as colored, nigger, negro, black, and African American. The term "American", as it is used by many conservatives often implies White Anglo Saxon Protestants only. The term does not include people of color and even excludes some Europeans such as "Jews".

The Constitution of the Nuwaubian Nation of Moors

The Constitution of the Nuwaubian Nation of Moors (Nuwaubian Nation) was officially published by Malachi Z. York, known then Chief Black Eagle, on June 26, 1992. This date is explicitly stated in the constitution itself and marks the formal establishment of the Nuwaubian Nation of Moors as an indigenous nation with its own governing laws and principles. The constitution asserts the legal and social framework for governance and operations within the community. It also emphasizes a distinct ethnic identity separate from American racial classifications. The constitution promotes the preservation and practice of Nuwaubian culture, language, and spiritual practices. It mandates education in the Nuwaubian language, ensuring that future generations would maintain a keen sense of their Nuwaubian identity. The constitution also asserts claims of sovereignty and hints at territorial rights, referencing various international declarations to support these claims. However, such assertions contend with domestic and internationally recognized laws and regulations.

The constitutional cornerstone of the Nuwaubian Nation faced significant challenges from its onset. It was hastily written and functionally irrelevant to the democratic form of governance it suggested. In reality, governance of the Nuwaubian Nation was hierarchical, theocratic, and authoritarian with York at the helm as the Supreme Grand Master. This top-down approach positioned York not only as political leader, but also as spiritual guide, creating a Theocratic Authoritarian community. It is both a declaration of independence and a guide for communal living according to York's unique blend of religious, cultural, and political aspirations.

The Constitution of the Nuwaubian Nation of Moors, as drafted by Malachi Z. York, diverges significantly from typical democratic constitutions. Unlike most democratic constitutions that emphasize a separation of powers, the Constitution of the Nuwaubian Nation of Moors centralized power around a single leader as the Maku or Supreme Grand Master. As a principle, democratic societies typically distribute power and implement checks and balances to prevent any one person or group from having excessive control. Further, the constitution of the Nuwaubian Nation of Moors extends beyond the typical legal framework and minimum moral standards (e.g., the illegality of theft or homicide) to dictate social behaviors and norms, which are reflective of the diverse cultures and backgrounds of a nation's citizenry. Further, typical democratic constitution's guarantee certain individual rights allowing for diverse cultural expressions and personal freedoms. The Constitution of Nuwaubian Nation of Moors, however, focuses heavily on community commitments and duties that align with the cultural and religious ethos of the Maku.

The Constitution of the Nuwaubian Nation of Moors also implores strong statements about the Nation's interactions with external authorities and governments. It insists on the recognition of the community's sovereign status and rejects external interference, both of which are normally backed by military might. This emphasis on sovereignty and self-governance brings to mind the complex interaction with the broader American and International legal landscapes which often leads to significant legal challenges and disputes. Constitutional democracies generally operate within internationally recognized geo-political boundaries and conform to a set of international norms and standards. Nevertheless, the Constitution of the Nuwaubian Nation of Moors represents a unique blend of theocratic governance, centralized authority, and deep cultural integration that stands in contrast to the pluralistic and often secular frameworks of democratic constitutions. Its approach highlights a community-centric governance model that prioritizes spiritual and cultural cohesion over the democratic values of individual rights and separation of powers.

Eatonton, GA

The Nuwaubian Nation of Moors established a community in Eatonton, GA, located seventy-eight miles southeast of Atlanta, situated a midst the hills and lakes of Putnam County. Eatonton can be characterized by its rustic charm, country roads flanked by cattle farms, fruit vendors, and lush forests. Eatonton is the birthplace of Joel Chandler Harris, author of the Uncle Remus tales, and Alice Walker, renowned author of The Color Purple. The city honors both Harris and Walker with dedicated museums. The Square of Downtown Eatonton is dominated by the county courthouse and a Confederate memorial, reflecting a deep-rooted antebellum heritage. In a small Bible-Belt confederate community, the arrival of a large, organized group of "black" people would naturally arouse the community's suspicion.

Yet, no one paid attention when a Brooklyn man named Malachi York purchased 476 acres on Shady Dale Road in Putnam County Georgia. However, when black cowboys sporting 10-gallon hats and boots began appearing in Eatonton (the seat of Putnam County Georgia), locals took notice. Originally perceived to be one large family, they were often referred to as the "York's". Despite the peculiar sight of black cowboys in Georgia, residents found themselves intrigued. When hundreds of "Yorks" began relocating to Eatonton from various cities across the country, questions arose as to the identity and intentions of these newcomers. Shortly after arriving to Eatonton, Malachi Z. York dubbed himself "Chief Black Eagle" designating the group the Yamassee Native Americans of the Creek Nation and applying for a license to operate a casino on the land. Articles soon appeared in the local newspapers that described the group as a "quasi-religious sect;" a gang of weird black guys with Brooklyn accents, who dressed up as cowboys, and pretended to be Indians. Who were these black Indians the Folks of Putnam County could not help wondering.

The people of Eatonton watched this activity with mixed feelings. Across the country, a series of new religious movements had erupted in tumultuous and highly publicized tragedies. The mass suicide of Jim Jones and his followers in Jonestown in 1978, the 1982 takeover of Antelope, Oregon, by Osho's red robed Rajneeshees, and the devastating siege of David Koresh's Branch Davidians compound in Waco, TX which resulted in the deaths of over eighty individuals. Each having a lingering impact in the psyche of most Americans old enough to recall any of these events. As the Nuwaubians entered the scene, the sight of fringe groups led by charismatic leaders raised suspicions among the media, the public, and law enforcement agencies.

Tama Re "Land of the Sun"

The first news reports portrayed the Nuwaubians in a light-hearted fashion as "simply bizarre." However, as construction on the land purchased by Malachi Z. York progressed, the media's portrayal of the Nuwaubians shifted from a lighthearted curiosity to a growing concern. The Nuwaubian Nation began to experience a series of legal and bureaucratic obstacles to its Utopian society as the media began to cast them in a more threatening light. "When they began talking about a mothership coming to take away 144,000 chosen ones...well, that's when people started to see them as an alien cult like Heaven's Gate" stated Sheriff Howard Sills of the Putnam County Sheriff's Department. According to Sills, calls flooded the Putnam County Sheriff's Department questioning the group's status and the potential for danger. Meanwhile, local journalists labeled Nuwaubians as "racist," and townspeople began referring to them as the "Waubs", reflecting the escalating tension and unease surrounding the group's presence in the small town.

Tama Re ("Land of the Sun") also known as "Egypt of the West, Wahanee, the Golden City, Kodesh or simply "The Land" embodied Malachi's vision of a physical and spiritual hub for Nuwaubian people. Its development commenced in the mid-nineties, spanning approximately 476 acres of land, aimed at creating a self-sufficient communal living space rooted in African culture. The compound served as a striking visual representation of this spiritual legacy. It provided a venue for Nuwaubian Moors to live by their principles, partake in religious and educational activities of their choosing, and celebrate their cultural identity. Tama Re hosted festivals, ceremonies, and educational events that attracted participants from across the United States and the world. Tama Re also functioned as a tourist attraction, pilgrimage site, and refuge for Nuwaubians throughout the United States anticipating the apocalypse as prophesized by York. Over the course of just a few years the landscape of the former diary pasture would evolve to feature notable Nuwaubian landmarks, including a forty-foot black pyramid

(Mir), statues of Egyptian deities, and other architectural elements symbolic of ancient Nile River Valley Civilizations.

As Tama Re grew the Nuwaubian Nation established bonds with the wider community. While the original Tents of Kedar maintained a toehold in Brooklyn—bookstores across the nation re-branded as All Eyes on Egipt, alluding to Tama Re. Malachi Z York established All Eyes on Egipt bookstores in various cities throughout the United States, where student teachers held free lessons on Nuwaubu, sold pamphlets, cassette tapes, video tapes, and novelties. York encouraged Nuwaubians to vote in local elections and take jobs in Putman and nearby counties. C. Jack Ellis, then mayor of Macon, GA began to drop by; so too did State Representative Tyrone Brooks from Atlanta. The annual "Savior's Day" celebration of Malachi Z. York birthday on June 26 opened Tama Re to the public, drawing thousands of visitors from across the United States and abroad. At its height in 1998 and 1999, more than five thousand individuals attended the annual event. Many visitors were pilgrims, some were the families of those living on Tama Re, others were simply curious.

The development of Tama Re faced numerous legal challenges and controversies. The Nation was at odds with local authorities and the community of Eatonton over concerns ranging from building codes to land use regulations, exacerbated by the presence of towering statues depicting African deities and 40-foot pyramids. 404 Shady Dale Road became the focus of intense scrutiny as escalating tensions eventually boiled over into legal action against Malachi Z. York and the Nuwaubian Nation of Moors. As hostility mounted, armed sentinels stood guard at the main gate (Pylon) adorned with Nuwaubian Egyptian figures, marking a stark change in the atmosphere of the land.

According to one former resident, issues began to surface when Putnam County officials realized that the newcomers were not merely a large family of "Yorks." As Nuwaubians from across the Nation began pouring into Putnam County, the building and land use applications evolved from a few isolated housing permits to multiple building permits and a rezoning application. At that time, the Nuwaubian Nation had purchased nearly a hundred mobile homes to accommodate families wishing to live together. However, the community was prevented from erecting these homes by the Putnam County Planning and Development authorities.

Others suggest that problems with county officials began shortly after the second annual Halloween party. A former general contractor for the Nuwaubian Nation of Moors, stated that upon hearing that Nuwaubians were operating a "nightclub" on the land county officials began acting to shut it down. Club Ramses, as it was named, was a social club for community members and alcohol was strictly prohibited in Tama Re. Club Rameses was used for community gatherings, social events, and ceremonies. According to several former residents of Tama Re, Sheriff Howard Sill attempted to unlawfully access Tama Re under the false pretense of building inspections. However, Sill was met at the Gate by armed guards and denied access, as it is not within the legal duties of a county sheriff to conduct building inspections.

Upon returning to Tama Re with an actual building inspector, Sheriff Sills was granted access to Tama Re, where they found the Rameses Social Club: an empty storage building wired with electricity and supposedly outfitted with catering. A month later, county officials shut down Rameses Social Club and padlocked the doors citing it as non-compliant with county building codes and operating without a certificate of occupancy. There were a few additional code violations, which county officials used as a justification to request an injunction; shutting down all other buildings on the land.

A contractor was hired by the Nuwaubian Nation to obtain a certificate of occupancy for Rameses Social Club. Although the contractor filed the necessary paperwork, once the injunction was in place county officials began denying all applications submitted by the Nuwaubian Nation of Moors. Despite the fact that Nuwaubians had owned the land prior to 1997 building code updates, county officials attempted to disrupt utility services to the land. This injunction included previously certified homes and offices, not just the non-compliant buildings. In response, Nuwaubians passed out pamphlets accusing Putnam County Commissioner Sandra Adams and other black officials of miscegenation.

Tensions had been simmering for some time when locals began to express a growing resentment toward the Nuwaubian Nation, whom they perceived as "arrogant." Nuwaubians complained about their neighbors' unwelcoming and intolerant attitudes. To make matters worse, York ignited a fire when he declared Tama Re a sovereign nation-state, requiring visitors to exchange their money for "Egiptian" coins and to purchase visas to cross over the borders of Tama Re. In 1997 and 1998, disagreements with white residents intensified over zoning permits and the arrival of thousands of black pilgrims for the annual week-long "Saviors' Day" festival. Conflict with local residents grew so intense that observers warned it could erupt into violence. Howard Sills, who was elected as sheriff just as York declared the property a sovereign state, challenged Nuwaubians over zoning, seeking to halt construction on the land. Nuwaubians pushed back by flooding the streets of Eatonton and surrounding Putnam County with newsletters excoriating municipal officials as racists.

Following a lengthy and arduous series of legal battles over land use and zoning, Malachi Z. York initiated a series of strategic maneuvers. He acquired a private residence in Athens, Georgia, transferred title of Tama Re, first to Tama Re Enterprises, and then onto a trust established for the benefit of Tama Re's residents. This move ensured that the benefits of the property would be preserved for the group. On February 21st, 2001, Malachi Z. York was cleared of all building and zoning infractions that had been issued since 1998. This exoneration, officially decreed by

Sheriff Howard Sills, put to rest the allegations of land-use improprieties that had been a source of contention between York and local authorities. At least it seemed that way at the time.

Prodigal Son

It was in early 2001 that Sheriff Howard Sills reportedly received a call from a man claiming to be the estranged son of Nuwaubian leader Malachi Z. York. At his request, Sills arranged to meet with him at the Atlanta FBI field office. It was during this meeting that Sheriff Howard Sills claims that York's son revealed to him how he had left the community in the nineties prior to their relocation to Georgia, due to his father's exploitation of the group for his personal gain and sexual abuse against young women. According to Sheriff Sills, he had several young women prepared to come forward.

Supposedly this caller was the son of Malachi Z. York and his late wife who had parted ways with the Ansaaru Allah Community in 1998. In the late 1990s York's son reportedly began to support groups of former Nuwaubian Moors who had left or been barred from Tama Re, apparently providing much needed financial assistance, moral support, and help reintegrating back into mainstream American society. This son eventually became aware of the existence of multiple half-siblings and suspected his father of inappropriate relationships with the young women of the community. According to Sills, this son explained how Malachi would start grooming Nuwaubian girls at a youthful age, eventually taking sexual advantage of them when they were teens and making them carry his babies until they got old, and he got bored. Then he would start over again with a new crop of girls. He speculated that Malachi Z. York may have fathered as many as one hundred illegitimate children.

Supposedly, he encouraged several ex-Nuwaubians who had given birth to his half-siblings to file for child support. He also began quietly gathering evidence about his father's sexual activities to hand over to the FBI and Sheriff Howard Sills. Up to this point the U.S. Federal Bureau of Investigations had been investigating Malachi Z. York and his organizations for nearly three decades with nothing indictable to show against Rev. Malachi Z. York nor the community as an organization. They had repeatedly tried to tie the organization to check kiting, burglary, financial fraud, gun running, arson, murder, and even domestic terrorism. It turns out that while some Nuwaubians may have been involved in illegal or immoral activities, none of it could be tied back to the organization nor Malachi Z. York.

2002 Arrest

The Putnam County Sheriff's Office worked with federal law enforcement to develop criminal charges against Malachi Z. York. On May 8, 2002, nearly three hundred federal agents from the F.B.I, ATF, and other government entities along with deputies from several Georgia law enforcement offices executed a military styled raid on the community of Tama Re. Agents and officers rammed through the gates in armored vehicles and descended on Tama Re from helicopters. Several different S.W.A.T. teams fanned out through the pyramids and trailers, going from building to building, as they methodically and systematically executed search warrants for each building. Law enforcement officials came prepared for the worst, bringing along evidence trailers, body bags, and freezer-trucks to preserve the remains of any would be Nuwaubians combatants. Fortunately, the majority of the community's men were away at work during the raid which was initially been planned for 3 a.m. A fortuitous delay prevented what would have likely resulted in a deadly nighttime surprise encounter.

Simultaneous operations were conducted at York's residence in Athens, Georgia. This secondary raid resulted in the arrest of several women, the seizure of financial documents later used in the federal structuring case, and the placement of five children into protective custody. Malachi Z. York was apprehended in the parking lot of a Milledgeville shopping center and charged with four felony counts of transporting minors across state lines for illicit purposes, each count carrying a maximum penalty of 15 years in prison and a $250,000 fine. As the raids unfolded, the overwhelming presence of tactically equipped agents and armored vehicles created an aura of intimidation. Far from the hundreds that they expected, law enforcement officials encountered slightly more than a hundred people, most of them women and children. The intent of the operation was revealed by the use of flash bangs and small-grade explosives that not only breached the peace but physically impacted residents, including a woman who suffered an asthma attack amid the chaos. In an unsettling display of force, children were compelled to kneel, with weapons aimed at their heads, while tear gas was deployed, adding to the distress. Despite the extensive manpower and preparation, the raids uncovered little, if any, evidence of criminal activities, there was no resistance, and no one was injured except Sheriff Sill who "got dehydrated at the end of the day, had to have a bag of fluids."

The disclosure of these charges led to a rapid withdrawal of support from high-profile individuals, including Jesse Jackson and Tyrone Brooks. These figures found themselves struggling to create distance from the group as the negative fallout spread. Most of their celebrity champions argued that they had nothing to do with the group, in an attempt to shield their reputations from the ensuing scandal. This was particularly true for Jesse Jackson, who had once gasconaded Tama Re as "the American Dream!" and now had to navigate the backlash from such a strong public endorsement. The entanglement with such an organization and the subsequent effort to dissociate with it highlighted the complex interplay between public support and personal reputation, especially when faced with sudden and damaging allegations.

The Trial

Malachi Z York was indicted as "Dwight" York under the Mann Act on four counts of transporting minors across state lines for illicit purposes! Named after Illinois Congressman James R. Man, the Mann Act, also known as the White-Slave Traffic Act, was enacted by Congress in 1910 to target pimps who transported women across state lines for the purposes of prostitution or debauchery. In reality, the law targeted black pimps trafficking white prostitutes. Hence, it is original name "the White-Slave Traffic Act of 1910." Those of you familiar with Robert Beck, also known as Iceberg Slim, may recall that Slim was incarcerated under the Mann Act. At the time of York's alleged crimes there existed no federal statutes on child molestation.

In addition to federal charges, Malachi Z. York was also facing criminal indictment by the State of Georgia. On May 14th, 2002, Malachi Z York was indicted by the State of Georgia on more than 120 counts of child molestation and rape. He would be indicted twice more by the State of Georgia over the same alleged acts. On August 2, 2002, the State of Georgia, assisted by District Attorney Fred Bright and Asst. District Attorney Dawn Baskin, convened a second grand jury hearing to indict Malachi Z. York for a second time. However, due to procedural irregularities the indictment was dismissed that same day. The State of Georgia unsealed a second superseding indictment against York on October 2, 2002, with 208 counts of child molestation.

In a letter drafted by Asst. District Attorney Richard Moultrie and sent to defense attorneys Edward Garland, Manubir Arora, and Frank A. Rubino federal prosecutor Attorney Max Wood and Asst. US Attorney Richard Moultrie made known their intentions to seek a second federal indictment. Then, on November 20, 2003, the United States Government superseded its then current indictment of four counts of Transporting Minors for the purpose of unlawful sexual activity and presented a new indictment to a grand jury in Macon, GA for violations of federal Racketeer Influence and Corrupt Organizations (RICO) statutes and the Mann Act. This superseding indictment alleged that the Nuwaubian Nation of Moors was established for the purposes of child molestation.

The indictments, accusing Rev. Malachi Z. York of various sexual crimes against minors outlined several instances of abuse that allegedly span the course of several years and across several state lines. The prosecution alleged that from 1993 through 2002 Malachi Z. York perpetrated more than eleven thousand five hundred individual acts of child molestation, aggravated child molestation, enticing a child for indecent purposes, statutory rape, and rape. The case against York was based largely on the strength of witness testimony, with 13 named victims and supposedly 200+ witnesses ready to testify against York. During preliminary hearing Judge Claude Hicks compared Malachi Z. York to the likes of Jim Jones from the Jonestown Massacre.

The defense moved to have the charges dismissed, disputing the court's jurisdiction, challenging the statutes of limitations, questioning the illegality of the alleged acts, and highlighting the absence of any physical evidence. A former Macon Police Office, who took a special interest in the case, suggested that most of the alleged acts were past a statute of limitations, even if they were true. Further, those not outside of a prosecutable statute of limitations were not illegal at the time the alleged acts took place. To make matters worse, many of the alleged victims and witnesses for the prosecution refused to cooperate. Nevertheless, despite the defense's argument the court proceeded with the case.

Other parties taken into custody with York on May 8th (all women) were apparently given the opportunity to turn witness or face prosecution as co-defendants; all but one refused to cooperate. The former Macon Officer who took a special interest in the case stated that there was evidence of official misconduct and procedural errors from day one of the grand jury indictment. He even went on to suggest that during the grand jury hearing prosecutors openly admitted to having no physical evidence nor eyewitnesses to substantiate York's alleged crimes of sexual molestation nor transporting, or causing to be transported, children across state lines for illicit purposes. Additionally, Judge Phil Spivey of the Jones County Ocmulgee Juvenile Circuit stated in court on July 17, 2002, that none of the children that were taken and placed into the custody of The Department of Family and Children Services (DFACS) had any signs of ever being molested.

During the early preliminary hearings attorneys' Ed Garland and Frank Rubino began pressuring Malachi Z. York to accept a plea deal. According to York, Garland depleted the organization's funds but failed to effectively counsel his Nuwaubian clients. It is said that altogether the Garland, Samuel, and Loeb firm received over $1.5MM from the Nuwaubian Nation of Moors to defend Malachi Z York and the five women taken into custody with him on May 8th. In a telephone interview from jail, York explains how Frank Rubino, Manny Arora, and Ed Garland of the Garland, Samuel, & Loeb firm ignored their clients, only visiting once to discuss money.

According to Malachi Z. York, Ed Garland consistently told him that it was impossible to win the case and that if he (York) were his son he would encourage him to take the deal. Garland questioned why York would allow the others apprehended with him on May 8th to suffer, when they would be released upon his acceptance of the deal. York detailed how he and the others were subjected to extreme sleep deprivation, starvation, physical & psychological abuse, and deprived of medication. The young children that were taken into protective custody were transported to an undisclosed location. All five were later proven by the State of Georgia to have never been sexually abused, yet they remained in protective custody.

The Plea

In January 2003, Malachi Z. York reluctantly agreed to plea deals on both the federal charges and state charges that would have limited his sentence. In exchange for a guilty plea, Malachi Z. York would forfeit some $400,000 in cash and other assets that had been seized during the raid, serve 15 years in Federal prison, register as a sex offender, and spend 36 years on probation. Although Malachi Z. York had upheld his end of the bargain by pleading guilty, US District Court Judge Hugh Lawson rejected the agreement four months later. Judge Lawson never explained his reason for throwing out the plea agreement and excused himself from the bench before the trial began.

In the United States legal system, a plea agreement or plea bargain between the defendant and the prosecution is not final until it receives approval from a judge. A judge has the authority to reject a plea deal for several reasons, even after a defendant agrees to sign a confession as part of the plea agreement. This judicial oversight was intended to serve as a check to ensure that plea agreements are in the interest of justice, fair to all parties, and not contrary to public policy. In the case of Malachi Z. York, the judge rejected the plea agreement for reasons that are under federal seal and have not been made public.

After the plea deal was rejected, York's defense team faced significant challenges. Forced to go to trial, the defense had not prepared a single witness in the weeks leading up to the trial. Dissatisfied, York filed a motion to be relieved of ineffective counsel. On December 15th, 2003, after the recusal of Judge Hugh Lawson, U.S. District Judge C. Ashley Royal inherited the York case. Judge Royal begrudgingly approved York's motion to replace his ineffective counsel. However, he refused to grant any extensions accusing Malachi Z. York of intentionally attempting to delay the trial. On December 17th, 2003, Adrian C. Patrick came on as new counsel for the defense. However, the trial was set for January 2004, giving lead attorney, Adrian Patrick, less than two months to prepare for a complex federal trial, a task made daunting by the voluminous case files and number of witnesses involved.

January 5th, 2004 marked the start of the Federal trial against Malachi Z. York. Due to negative publicity, the trial was held in presiding Judge C. Ashley Royal's hometown of Brunswick, Georgia. During the trial several of the alleged victims took the stand to deny the allegations of abuse and other witnesses refused to testify. In fact, the defense called some of the alleged victims, named in the indictment, to testify on behalf of Malachi Z York, all who maintained that nothing ever happened and that he was innocent. This led to questions about the credibility of the prosecution's case. Altogether, there were thirteen named victims, five of which were taken into DFACS custody during the May 8th raid on Tama Re, and subsequently rules by Judge Spivey to have never been molested. Of the eight remaining alleged victims, three recanted their statements and two were never subpoenaed to appear in court.

Prosecutors claimed to have in excess of two hundreds witnesses against Malachi Z. York. Nearly three-quarters of the prosecution's witnesses were active employees on the payroll of the Federal Bureau of Investigation or other government agencies. However, during the trial federal prosecutors only called on forty-seven witnesses, mostly FBI agents. Considering Judge Spivey's ruling the prosecution only had eight named victims, three of which had recanted their testimony, and two who were never subpoenaed to appear in court. Every witness for the defense, including those named as victims in the indictment, adamantly denied all allegations of molestation or having ever seen anyone else being molested. The Defense called on eight of the prosecution's named victims; all eight denied having ever been molested by Malachi Z. York. Those alleged victims called on by the defense testified that they traveled with their parents or others, but not with Malachi York. They also testified that Malachi Z York never ordered anyone to travel to Georgia from New York. Further, the mother, brother, and best friends of one alleged victim testified under oath that she admitted to falsely conspiring against Malachi Z. York. Still another witness came forward to testify about an alleged conspiracy against Malachi Z. York, on a trip to South Beach with York's estranged son where the plot was formed. It has been suggested that several of the alleged victims/witnesses lived in the house and had sexual relationships with this son who was reportedly upset with his father over money and that this is why he went to the Federal Government.

The defense also questioned the lack of any physical evidence. Out of eleven thousand five hundred alleged sexual encounters there existed no physical evidence, DNA evidence, audio, picture, nor video evidence. Although the Federal Bureau of Investigation claimed to have been investigating Malachi Z. York and the Nuwaubian Nation of Moors for more than two decades, no video or audio surveillance was produced during the trial. Neil Dukoff, Malachi York's tax accountant, whose father was York's accountant for more than 30 years prior to that, testified that from 1996 to 2001 Malachi Z York reported well over 1 MILLION dollars in taxes for each year. He also testified that Malachi Z York paid more in taxes than he should have for each of those years. Malachi Z York was never audited by the IRS nor received any notice of unpaid or delinquent taxes from the U.S. Internal Revenue Service.

The Verdict

The witness recantations and the circumstances under which they were made have been a major point of contention and part of the broader narrative arguing York's innocence and claim that he was the target of a conspiracy and wrongful prosecution. Supporters argue these recantations bolster their assertions that the charges against York were fabricated and that he was unjustly convicted. Throughout the legal proceedings, York and his defense team contended that the accusations were part of a broader governmental conspiracy to dismantle the Nuwaubian Nation, citing cultural and political motivations, rather than legal grounds. Objectively, I must call out the fact that recantations in cases of sexual abuse, especially those involving minors, are complex and can be influenced by numerous factors, including emotional and psychological pressures, loyalty to the accused, or fear of retribution.

Upon deciding the initial verdict, the jury was hung! However, in a matter of one hour the sole dissenting juror was persuaded to bring down a guilty verdict. The dissenting juror, number 62, maintained that Malachi Z York was set up and that she had heard of another case where someone was found guilty that was actually innocent. Despite the strength of the case presented by the defense, a guilty verdict came down on ten of the eleven counts against Malachi Z York. The jury found York guilty on multiple charges, including racketeering and transporting minors across state lines for illicit purposes. This verdict came after the hung jury was re-charged by the judge, a move that highlighted the contentious nature of the trial.

In the aftermath of the trial, the case continued to evoke strong reactions. More witnesses recanted their statements, and new information became known that further questioned the integrity of the legal process. The case of Malachi Z. York remains a focal point for discussions on judicial conduct, witness credibility, and the challenges of defending high-profile defendants charged with criminal cases in federal courts. Following his trial, York was sentenced to 135 years in prison. York's appeals have been unsuccessful in overturning his conviction. Reports have since emerged that a few of the individuals who had testified about being victims of abuse by York were coerced. These individuals reportedly claimed that they were pressured into making statements against York by law enforcement officials, family members, or due to the broader societal and community pressures surrounding the case.

Following York's sentencing, prosecutors requested that trial transcripts be sealed to protect the identity of minors and witnesses who testified against Malachi Z. York. However, Judge C. Ashley Royal went beyond that, having the entire document sealed from the public. It is likely that Malachi Z. York will spend the rest of his life in prison. York's arrest and conviction were a significant turning point for the Nuwaubian Nation of Moors. Following these events, the group has faced increased scrutiny, and Tama Re was eventually seized, demolished, and sold by the government.

Today

Today, Malachi Z. York (age 79) is currently serving out a 135-year prison sentence in ADX Florence Administrative Maximum Security Federal Prison which houses some of the world's most dangerous criminals, including Joaquin "El Chapo" Guzman Loera and Theodore Kaczynski also known as the Unabomber. He is in isolation 24 hours a day, barred from writing books or letters, and prohibited from any form of contact with the outside world, excluding his legal counsel and immediate family. 404 Shady Dale Road is now the home of White Oak Plantation, an executive retreat, recently sold by White Oak Plantation and Farms, LLC., a company built on a legacy of slavery in Baton Rouge, LA.

The victims have navigated various paths in the aftermath of the legal proceedings that led to York's conviction. Given the sensitivity and privacy concerns surrounding the victims, especially those who were minors at the time, we will forgo specific details about their individual journeys and current circumstances. However, it is important that we touch on the impact and broader implications for victims of abuse.

Victims of sexual abuse, particularly children, often experience significant psychological and emotional repercussions. These repercussions often include trauma, depression, anxiety, difficulty forming relationships, and struggles with self-esteem and identity. The public nature of the cases, involving figures like York, who was both a religious leader and a father figure to many, likely compounded the complexity of the victims' experiences and their healing processes. The road to recovery from abuse is highly personal and can be long and challenging. Victims may seek therapy and counseling, engage in support groups, or find solace in creative expression, advocacy, or community service. Some survivors of abuse become advocates for others who have experienced similar traumas, dedicating themselves to raising awareness, supporting healing, and preventing future abuse. Many victims choose to maintain their privacy and focus on rebuilding their lives away from the public eye. This may involve pursuing education, careers, and personal relationships, all while navigating the ongoing process of healing. The privacy and dignity of survivors are paramount, and their choices in how to move forward and heal deserve respect and support.

Personal Statement

To be clear, I am not arguing for, nor against, allegations of abuse and child molestation by Malachi Z. York. Only those parties directly involved know the unadulterated truth of what happened. However, I will say that if Malachi Z. York perpetrated the acts for which he has been accused, and subsequently found guilty by a court of law, then some form of justice has been served. If not, I sympathize for those who have conspired against an innocent man. Nevertheless, my purpose in approaching this matter strictly relates to my interest in preserving the legacy of Nuwaubu and highlighting the disreputable circumstances that are often present in cases involving high profile revolutionary leaders of the Nuwaubian community. Undoubtedly, this book will upset some. Although this is not my intention, I am compelled to share this information with the community at this time.

16

The Messiah Complex

Throughout the years I have been aligned with various groups & organizations, each serving some specific purpose in constructing my road map to mental, spiritual, and social liberation. Although my individual experiences have been pleasant, others have not been so lucky. What I have noticed is that each of these organizations, like most other organizations, are plagued by scandal at some point in their existence. Most often, the scandals center around money, the direction of the organization, or the inappropriate behavior of some person in a position of power. Although some organizations have endured once scandal breaks most have been rocked to their core and are never quite the same.

In the Nuwaubian community, there are two broad domains in which leadership interacts with the Nuwaubian citizenry. The first broad domain of leadership rest within some range of tolerance by the broader American society. This does not necessarily mean that this domain of leadership is unassailable or immune to persecution. As history has often shown us, even the most benign of Nuwaubian leaders have been falsely imprisoned, maligned, and slain. Within acceptable domains such as American government, education, healthcare, media, finance, and scientific institutions, Nuwaubian leaderships tends to more or less safe from false imprisonment and murder. The second domain of interaction consists of community politics, history, culture, law, advocacy and religion. Unless sanctioned by the broader American society, leadership within these domains tend to face severe ridicule, ostracism, and assault. The methods of assault are not limited to physical belabour but also include defamation, suspicion, malicious prosecution, and persecution.

It is within these unsanctioned political, historical, cultural, legal, advocacy, and religious domains that Nuwaubian leadership tends to manifest itself mostly in the form of Theocratic Authoritarianism. That is not to say that organizations within these domains are not sincere in their purpose, just that they have been governed by antediluvian approaches to governance. These organizations are often steered by a few individuals, designated through some irreproachable authority, creating an aurora of forced conformance or isolation. They are often repressive in that they do not reflect the will of the people they claim to serve! The prevalence of such organizations speaks to the psychological conditioning that Nuwaubian people have suffered here in America. Most of us would readily trade liberty for "salvation" without ever questioning whether liberty is the salvation that we need.

Theocratic Authoritarianism

Theocratic Authoritarianism is an amalgamation of the concepts of Theocracy and Authoritarianism. It can be defined as: 1) a theocracy, a governance structure that is ruled by, or subjected to, religious authority and 2) authoritarianism, characterized by or favoring absolute obedience to authority at the expense of individual freedom. Some would argue that at times, religious leadership within Nuwaubian communities resembles absolute religious dictatorship. This form of Theocratic Authoritarianism often appears under the guise of a religious leader with a common recurring message: "Your current suffering (as descendants of enslaved persons, poverty, etc.) is due to some sin committed by you or your ancestors. To free yourself from this hellish experience, you must completely surrender your will to me or the power that speaks through me." This narrative is reminiscent of the justifications used by southern slave owners in America, who claimed that the ancestors' sins justified their descendants' enslavement and abuse. Thus, the only path to freedom was through total submission.

Messiah Complex

At the helm of theocratic authoritarian organizations, a messiah complex often emerges. A messiah complex can be described as a mental state in which a person believes they are the messiah, or a prophet sent to redeem humanity through some divine endeavor. It can also describe someone who believes they are responsible for helping or saving others. The messiah complex reflects the thought process of a person operating under the belief that they are 'found' and possess (or are a channel of access to) exclusive divine information that others need in order to obtain salvation, liberation, or some other divine right. They may perceive themselves as having unique insights or abilities that set them apart from others and make them uniquely qualified to lead or save humanity. This complex can appear in religious, political, or personal contexts, often leading to manipulative, controlling, or delusional behavior. Simply put, a person with a messiah complex view themselves as being enlightened, and others as wantonly lost. This is not to say that these particular individuals harbor some ulterior motive or have malevolent intentions. They may in fact possess some divinely inspired, or at least critical, information that would greatly benefit the community or humanity as a whole. Nevertheless, it does not necessarily follow that the community nor the whole of humanity should blindly follow one person. We must learn to recognize and value the individual strengths and weaknesses of our leaders without deifying them.

Novel Religious and Social Phenomena

Occasionally, particularly charismatic and messianic personalities with the ability to amass large followings emerge, resulting in New Religious Movements (NRM's) such as the Moorish Science Temple of America, Nation of Yahweh, or Nuwaubian Nation of Moors. Charismatic leaders like Malachi Z. York "who by force of their personalities are capable of having profound and extraordinary effects on their followers," are particularly skilled in amassing these large followings. The organizations sustained growth and progress becomes solely dependent on this single personality. When scandal is introduced, or the figured head is attacked, the organization is rendered ineffective. Normally, the damage suffered is beyond repair. However, there are examples of theocratic authoritarian organizations that have survived such scandal. For example, The Nation of Islam, under the leadership of Honorable Elijah Muhammad, was plagued by allegations of Elijah Muhammad's extramarital affairs with underage girls. This, along with a very public rift between, and eventual assassination of, El Hajj Malik El Shabazz worked to diminish the influence and reputation of the NOI in the mid-60's. Nevertheless, through the leadership of the Honorable Minister Louis Farrakhan, another charismatic leader, the Nation of Islam endures to this very day.

One Man's Ego

During my journey with Nuwaubu I have had the pleasure of establishing relationships with various members of the Original and New Black Panther Party (NBPP). Much like its predecessor, the New Black Panther Party has been plagued by scandal and division. As a student of the Original Black Panther Party for Self Defense I was always extremely cautious about formally establishing a relationship with the NBPP. Having studied the Black Panther Party since my adolescent years I am remarkably familiar with the tactics used by state and federal law enforcement to unjustly criminalize and neutralize the organization. By the time I finally decided to align myself with the NBPP it had splintered into various factions operating independently of one another, even within the same city and at times openly hostile toward one another. I chose to align myself with a particular faction of the Party, not because I preferred this group above the others, but because at the time that I was ready to join they were visible, actively recruiting, and operating within the community in which I lived.

Shortly after fulfilling my financial obligation and attending my first few regular meetings, I began to feel that the organization's purpose had been oversold. I am not suggesting that the organization's members had oversold its purpose, it is likely that I oversold the purpose of the organization to myself. I realized that although I do not know everything there is to know about the struggles of Nuwaubian people here in the Diaspora of North America, there is not much in the way of a basic history lessons that anyone could teach me that would fundamentally alter my thought process or change the direction of my life. My purpose in joining the organizations was not to be indoctrinated in religious dogma nor to better equip myself for street corner proselytization. I was not in search of a teacher nor a lesson in history, religion, politics, or etymology. My purpose in joining was purely the defense of Nuwaubian communities in the event of aggression against the community itself. My core values and direction in life were already well informed.

The Security and wellbeing of the community should be the number one priority for any paramilitary organization founded on the principle of defending Nuwaubian communities from outside aggression. To me, it seemed that this particular faction was focused more on garnering political influence and military postering than developing strategic responses to outside aggression and widespread catastrophe. I would never advocate for anyone to show up at emotionally charged, highly politized events with loaded firearms in protest as a show of force. It is dangerous and nothing more than peacocking. For the moment, let us suppose that a trained militia (e.g., Oath Keepers, Proud Boys, or Atomwaffen) decided to stage an assault and physically confront a group of non-combat ready protesters with live firearms. The resulting loss of life, liberty, or property would be tragic. It would also rest squarely on the shoulders of leadership.

Most protest would not involve any threat of serious bodily injury or death without the introduction of firearms. Armed protests as a shock tactic are not about the security and wellbeing of the community, they are about ego and very ineffective as far as civil disobedience is concerned. Any paramilitary organization founded on the purpose of defending Nuwaubian communities from outside aggression, should be controlled by Nuwaubian communities, not one nor a small group of individuals. Personally, I would like to see all paramilitary organizations, such as the New Black Panther Party or the NFAC, turned over to the control of the communities in which they operate. Members should have the ability to elect their own leadership. However, leadership should be subject to the oversight of a body elected by the broader Nuwaubian community. I believe that this type of an approach would increase participation from the community, as the community itself would have an active voice in the direction of the organization through the power of their vote. It would also increase visibility within the community, foster goodwill, and ensure that the organization stays within the bounds of the community it claims to represent and serve. Protests are civil, not military, actions. We should all hope that the distinct line between these two is never blurred.

Secular vs Non-Secular Organizations

When authoritarian governance and Messiah Complexes are combined with religion and politics it creates a rigid environment in which freedom of thought and expressions are stifled and the self-interest of those steering the organization grows unchecked. When I began my personal journey with Nuwaubu, I was often mis-labeled an atheist. Not because I denied the existence of divine powers in the universe but because my views differed from those of my Southern Baptist family and friends. As stated by Dr. Ray Hagins, "whenever people ask do you believe in God, what they are really asking is do you believe what they believe about God."

As a child growing up in the Bible Belt State of Arkansas, I was con-ditioned to view the word "secular" with a negative connotation. Most Christians would interpret the word secular as "worldly" and "against God." It was not until I was at odds when my own family and friends over my evolving religious beliefs that I realized even laical things have a divine purpose. The First Amendment of the United States Constitu-tion prohibits Congress from making any law that prioritizes any one re-ligion above another. The authors of the Constitution exercised divine foresight in their diligence to ensure that no overzealous religious leaders would hijack the future direction of the democratic experiment. Secular institutions provide neutral ground for people of varying religious be-liefs to set aside their differences and align on the pursuit of a common interest. Religious opinion has no official place in a truly democratic so-ciety. NUWAUBU IS NOT A RELIGION! Anyone that is promoting it as such is wrong.

Diversity of Thought

In Houston I would often wake up early on Saturday morning to visit the Buy Black Market Place at the Shrine of the Black Madonna. One Saturday, as I was walking back to my car after making my usual pur-chase of books, novelties, and supplements I was stopped by a brother with dreadlocks. He looked as if he could be close to my age, wore a Black Power Fist t-shirt, a beaded necklace, and several wrist bands. I stopped him as he began running down to me how "White Men" had deceived the black community into its current state. My assumption is that this brother took me as uninformed because I was wearing a fraternity t-shirt, jeans, and polo boots. I explained to him that I did not need a history lesson as I had been a Nuwaubian since 1997. He looked at me and said "Nuwaubian? Don't you think it is about time to let go of religion?" To which I replied, "hmm, I'm not religious at all." We exchanged awkward looks as we both went our separate ways.

Malachi Z. York always adamant about Nuwaubu not being a religion. As previously defined, Nuwaubu is the Science of Sound Right Reason through Right Knowledge, Right Wisdom, and Right Overstanding. Nevertheless, the divisiveness of religious dogma, messianic complexes, and scandal have diminished its reputation to the point where even the most devoted Nuwaubian have abandoned its name and cause. What I realized from my interaction with this random brother at the Shrine of the Black Madonna was that although I myself am far from religious, there are many so-called "Nuwaubians" who have, in effect, traded one religion and one master for another. Whether it is Christianity, Islam, Judaism, or the Anunnaki based religion of Ancient Summer, what these religious dogmas all have in common is that the overwhelming majority their parabolic tales cannot be substantiated outside of their respective religious text. That is okay! People are entitled to believe in whatsoever they choose. However, when it comes to our collective civil affairs must agree to the first universal law of mankind that every individual is entitled to their own beliefs, provided that those beliefs do not infringe upon the rights, safety, and wellbeing of another.

Over the years, I have watched many "Nuwaubians" antagonize members of the Nation of Islam, Moorish Science Temple of America, Black Hebrew Israelites, Christians, and members of various systems of belief using the teachings of Malachi Z. York. Not to advance overstanding and truth, but to belittle and destroy their system of beliefs, believing that they are emulating the style and charisma of the Master Teacher. I cannot recall any of these individuals ever turning that critical eye toward the "Holy Tablets". Had they done so, they would have quickly realized that like most other religious texts, its parabolic tales cannot be substantiated outside of the religious text itself.

Not one of these aspiring leaders has exhibited wisdom enough to empower the people they claim to represent and serve. Their egos have allowed feelings of animosity to grow and fester between Nuwaubians of various backgrounds and beliefs. There are many qualified leaders in the Nuwaubian community. Why would any self-respecting, highly educated, high performing individual acquiesce to one individual's delusions of self-grandeur? Nuwaubians are not in need of another leader, we need organization. There will only ever be one Malachi Z. York, and he was the intellectual and spiritual leaders many needed in that day and time (Hence the Man of the Hour).

17

The Beginning

The sudden incarceration of Malachi Z. York left the Nuwaubian Nation of Moors in state of total disarray. Many Nuwaubians that lived on Tama Re returned to their places of origin. Some who had previously identified as Nuwaubian joined the Moorish Science Temple of America and other Black Nationalist/Black Liberation groups. Like most other organizations before it, the sudden displacement of leadership created a power vacuum within the Nation leading to various factions, often openly hostile toward one another. Some remained steadfast in their allegiance to York's original teachings of Nuwaubu. Others became Nuwaupians and eventually Sabaeans. Nuwaubu transitioned to Nuwaupu, then to Wu Nuwaupu. The Nuwaubian Language morphed into Nuwaupuyee. New series of scrolls such as the Actual Facts Series, The Master Series, and Paa Taraq (The Way or the Path) were released while Malachi Z. York was imprisoned. Being that his writing privileges had been terminated, many took these writings as imposturous.

As a student of Nuwaubu and many other doctrines and philosophies I was never inclined to blindly follow the pack nor anyone individual. However, I must express the level of respect that I have for Malachi Z. York. I am certain that his teachings are a major component in the development of the person that I am today. Although I am not perfect, I am proud of the person that I am and of the things that I have accomplished. However, at some point after his incarceration, the teachings being published began to feel foreign to me. Naturally, I was inclined to continue with the original teachings and to align myself with individuals who shared similar views. Eventually, I would go on to work with several aspiring "leaders" with the intention of rebuilding this Nuwaubian dream turned nightmare.

Prior to collaborating with these individuals, I always made It clear that "just as I came on my own free will and accord, I will leave on my own free will and accord." Although my initial encounter with the teachings of Malachi Z. York awakened a natural curiosity and desire for knowledge that had laid dormant since my early adolescent years, it had never been the only teachings that I studied. I would wholeheartedly contribute to resurrecting what I felt was the closest things to our true African heritage and culture here in America. However, I refused to reduce myself to the sycophant of some egotistical despot.

Nuwaubian Excellence

In 2024, the National Urban League published its annual State of "Black" America Report, revealing progress in Nuwaubian representation in various factions of American civic life. Particularly in American politics, the number of Nuwaubian lawmakers has more than doubled since the start of the 1990's, reflecting advancement in political representation. Nuwaubians have also made significant strides economically since the nineties, with a lower poverty rate of 18.8% in 2019 compared to about half in 1966 (The National Urban League 2019). Despite improvements, about eight million Nuwaubians still live in poverty, according to the latest US Census Bureau report. The wealth gap between white and Nuwaubian families persists, with the average white family having nearly seven times more wealth than a Nuwaubian family as of 2019. Inheritances contribute to generational wealth discrepancies, affecting the ability to pass down assets through Nuwaubian families.

The study on which the report was based also revealed that the percentage of Nuwaubian completing four years of higher education increased to 26% in 2019 compared to just 4% in 1962. This growth underscores considerable progress in bachelor's, master's, and professional degree attainment. Enrollments in both college and graduate programs have reached historic highs, demonstrating ongoing advancement. Business management remains the top major among Nuwaubian, followed closely by the social sciences. Nuwaubians have an increasing presence in the fields of Science, Technology, Engineering, and Mathematics (STEM). The percentage of Nuwaubians earning professional degrees in Law, Medicine, Pharmacy and Divinity is also increasing. At no other point in our history has the Nuwaubian community possessed such a diverse level of talent.

Marshalling our Collective Talents

With such a diverse range of talent within the Nuwaubian community, how one could be so naïve, or arrogant, as to believe themselves superior to the group of which they are a part is bewildering. Regardless of your individual level of success, you can never rise above the group in which you are apart. Nevertheless, some of the least successful of us seem to think they have it all figured out. Not because of what they have discovered for themselves. But because of what they have been led to believe.

Today our community is under threat from far-right extremist and MAGA republicans who are advancing their ultra conservative agenda despite resistance from a majority of Americans. Republican controlled state legislators are positioning themselves to usurp power by circumventing the democratic process. Since the 2013 supreme court decision in the case of Shelby County vs. Holder, 570 U.S. 529 at least 29 states have enacted restrictive voting laws. Shelby County vs. Holder was a landmark case on the constitutionality of two provisions of the Voting Rights Act of 1965. When congress enacted the Voting Rights Act of

1965, it determined that racial discrimination in voting had been more prevalent in certain areas of the country. Section 4(a) of the Act established a formula to identify those areas and to provide for more stringent remedies where appropriate. Under Section 4(a) literacy test and other devices, as a prerequisite to voter registration where prohibited. Section 4(a) also guaranteed the right to register and vote for those with limited English proficiency and education. Section 5 of the Act required that any changes affecting voting in areas covered under section 4(a) be subject to review by either the U.S. District Court of D.C. or the U.S. Attorney General. In 2013, Section 4(a) was ruled to by unconstitutional by the U.S. Supreme Court.

The first wave of restrictive laws following the Shelby County vs. Holder supreme court decision were largely focused on imposing strict voter ID requirements. To be clear, most Americans are not opposed to protecting the integrity of the ballot box by requiring voters to present identification. However, these voter ID requirements went beyond requiring voters to present ID to restricting the types of acceptable ID's and the process for casting provisional ballots in the absence of identification. State lawmakers have also targeted vote-by-mail alternatives. Since the U.S. Supreme Court ruling on Shelby County vs. Holder, twenty-two states have passed forty-three such laws, thirty-three of which have been passed since the 2020 election. In the State of Texas, to be eligible to vote early by mail you must be 65 years or older, sick or disabled, out of the country on election day and during the period for early voting by personal appearance, expected to give birth within three weeks before or after election day, or be incarcerated but otherwise eligible to vote.

Current Threat

As you are reading this book, the legacy of our ancestors is being systematically erased from school history books and removed from public libraries. According to PEN America, a literary and free expression advocacy organization, between July 2021 and March 2022 1,586 books were banned in various states across the U.S., with Texas leading the charge, banning a total of 713 books across 16 different school districts (Friedman and Johnson 2022). To be fair, literary censorship is nothing new to America! In the first half of the 19th century, literature related to slavery alarmed southern slave owners. By the 1850s, multiple states had outlawed expressing anti-slavery sentiments, which abolitionist author Harriet Beecher Stowe defied in 1851 with the publication of Uncle Tom's Cabin. The book was publicly burned and banned by slaveholders along with other anti-slavery books. In Maryland, free black minister Sam Green was sentenced to 10 years in the state penitentiary for owning a copy of the book.

As the Civil War raged in the 1860s, the pro-slavery South continued to ban abolitionist materials while Union authorities banned pro-Southern literature like John Cook's biography of Confederate General Stonewall Jackson. In 1873, the war against books went federal with the passage of the Comstock Act, a law that made it illegal to possess "obscene" or "immoral" texts or articles or send them through the mail. These laws in particular were designed to ban both content about sexuality and birth control, which at the time were widely available via mail order. The Jim Crow-era South was a particular hotbed for book censorship. The United Daughters of the Confederacy made several successful attempts to ban school textbooks that did not offer a sympathetic view of the South's loss in the Civil War.

In 1969, the Supreme Court weighed in on students' right to free expression. In Tinker v. Des Moines, a case involving students who wore black armbands protesting the Vietnam War to school, the court ruled 7-2 that "neither teachers nor students shed their constitutional rights to freedom of speech or expression at the schoolhouse gate." In 1982, the Supreme Court overtly addressed schoolbooks in a case involving a group of students who sued a New York school board for removing books by authors like Kurt Vonnegut and Langston Hughes that the board deemed "anti-American, anti-Christian, anti-Semitic, and just plain filthy." "Local school boards may not remove books from school libraries simply because they dislike the ideas contained in those books," the court ruled in Island Trees Union Free School District v. Pico, citing students' First Amendment rights.

If we cannot read the gigantic print on the wall at this point, I am not sure there is any hope. As an ethnic group, we are currently faced with a choice. We must either learn to work together toward establishing an insular sub-society or perish as other ethnic groups synergize and advance their own interest. Regardless of our individual social class, sexual orientation, gender identification, beliefs, heritage, language, or culture we are identified by ourselves and others as a single ethnic group. I do not recall ever hearing the slave owners of America's dark past inquiring as to whether or not our ancestors were male or female, Judeo-Christian, or Muslim, or whether they spoke certain languages prior to enslaving them. Nor do I recall any of our ancestors being asked what hood they were from prior to being lynch. The prerequisite for being enslaved, lynched, raped, abused, and oppressed was purely based on one factor and one factor alone, our African lineage as evidenced by the hue of our skin. The reason that African American gangsters adorn different colors is to fabricate a differentiation where there is none, as we are all reflections of the same homogeneous group. We are in this together whether we choose to accept that fact or not. The only question that remains is whether we will survive and thrive together, or parish together.

The Big Ask

At this point I do not feel the need to be coy nor timid about exactly what it is that I would like from my audience. My desire is for Nuwaubian people (African Americans, Creoles, Geaches, Moors, Moabites, Black Hebrew Israelites, etc.) in America from varying backgrounds and beliefs (Christianity, Islam, Judaism, Sikhs, Atheist, etc.) to assemble and form a singular ethnic nation. By ethnic nation, I do not mean an ethnic nation-state, as in a political unit consisting of an autonomous state inhabited, predominantly, by a particular ethnic group. It is not reasonable an aspiration to establish an autonomous nation-state within the recognized borders of an established state. This is not only a violation of international laws, but also a threat to the safety and security of that state. That is not to say that we cannot have that one day. However, we are definitely not ready, nor in a position, to operate at such a level on the world stage. We cannot even cooperate in an environment surrounded by oppressive forces, a situation that would normally unite a people. By ethnic nation I mean a distinct body of people, internally and externally recognized; sufficiently conscious of their unity and identity; striving to determine their own destiny and govern the civic affairs of their own community.

Regardless of whether we choose to accept it, we are already externally recognized as a single ethnic nation. For many Americans, we are African by ethnicity and American in citizenship only. This is why the mention of "American People" by certain politicians does not include nor considered the interest of people of color. Likewise, most Africans, including the Moors of Morocco, would consider us as American. We are the descendants of Americas former slave population, stripped of our cultural identities and heritage; not quite American, not quite African, but somewhere in between. Every ethnic group in America can trace its lineage back to a specific place and people; Irish, Italian, English, Chinese, Vietnamese, Korean, Mexican, Cuban, Cherokee, Choctaw. Everyone, but Americas most deserving group of people. As a young man I learned to view obstacles, as opportunities. Opportunities to prove to myself and to the world that I could not only rise to the challenge, but that I could do so with integrity and grace. This is our chance to prove to ourselves and to the world that we cannot only rise to the challenge, but that we can do so in a manner befitting of the Owners,

Makers, Cream of the Planet, Farther and Mothers of Civilization and Gods of the Universe. For all intents and purposes, we are a new people, new beings, Nuwaubians. Although race relations in America have improved some over the past century, a substantial portion of white Americans are still unwilling to truly accept unless us as citizens of this country we acquiesce to their opinions of who they think we should be. Today they are overtly peeling back all of the hard-fought rights that we have earned in this country.

What are the benefits of an ethnic identity

There are numerous cultural, social, and political benefits associated with the adoption of a distinct ethnic identity (Nuwaubian). A collective ethnic identity would serve as a vehicle for preserving our cultural heritage, traditions, languages, and customs. The preservation of these cultural heirlooms is critical for the maintenance and continuity of our cultural identity across generations. A distinct ethnic identity can also foster a sense of pride and solidarity among Nuwaubian youth, reduce feelings of alienation and isolation, promote social cohesion and mutual support within the community. Further, a single ethnic identity would serve as a platform for Nuwaubian people to demand recognition and representation within the context of the broader American culture; ultimately leading to greater participation and influence within the broader American political system.

Ethnic identities often create bonds that can strengthen social ties and cooperation among its members. I have often heard our people ask, how it is that other races come to the U.S. and prosper, yet we who have given our freedom and lives to this country suffer without acknowledgment, let alone reward. My conjecture is that one of the primary reasons we are unable to excel as a people is because we have no true ethnic identity outside of the one that America has created for us. As far as identities are concerned, those that provide us with a sense of pride and self-worth are normally those that we choose for ourselves. Those identities heaped upon us by others are usually derogatory and work toward undermining our sense of dignity and self-worth.

Ethnic nations contribute to the diversity of human culture and society, enriching the global tapestry of tradition, perspective, and experience. Celebrating and preserving ethnic diversity is essential for fostering mutual understanding and tolerance between the various ethnicities of the human family. Ethnic nations often engage in cultural exchange with other ethnic groups, fostering mutual understanding, cooperation, and appreciation for diverse cultures. This exchange can lead to innovation, creativity, and the enrichment of collective knowledge.

The Beginning

I am looking to organize, empower, and energize Nuwaubian people. We will always be the descendants of African slaves, and Africa will always be a part of us. But we are a new people, Nuwaubians, bound together by the unique legacy of our ancestors. This is the opportunity for us to write a new legacy. If you agree, I simply ask that you sign our petition to be formally recognized in America and by the rest of the world as Nuwaubian. Not colored, not negro, not African American. I Am Nuwaubian!

Please sign our petition!

Bibliography

Aldwin, Carolyn, Heidi Igarashi, and Michael Levenson. 2018. "The Development of Wisdom: A Social Ecological Approach." *The Journal of Gerontology: Series B, Volume 73, Issue 8* 1350-1358.

Amen, Rkhty. 2019. *The Writing System of Medu Neter.* Independently Published.

Anthony, Jr. , Marshall, Howard Howard Nichols, and Wil Del Pilar. 2021. "Raising Undergraduate Degree Attainment Among Black Women and Men Takes on New Urgency Amid the Pandemic." *The Education Trust.* May 13. Accessed July 6, 2024. https://edtrust.org/resource/national-and-state-degree-attainment-for-black-women-and-men/#:~:text=Our%20previous%20work%20identified%20a%2017%20percent-age%20point,Black%20women.%20That%E2%80%99s%20a%2015%20percentage%2 0point%20gap.

Archives at Tuskegee Institute. n.d. "Lynchings: By Year and Race." *University of Missouri-Kansas City.* Accessed July 7, 2024. http://law2.umkc.edu/faculty/projects/ftrials/shipp/lynchingyear.html.

Beekes, Ph.D., Robert, and Lucien van Beek, Ph.D. 2016. *Etymological dictionary of Greek.* Brill.

Bracher, Mark. 2021. "Foundations of a Wisdom-Cultivating Pedagogy: Developing Systems Thinking across the University Disciplines." *Philosophies; Basel Vol. 6, Iss. 3,* .

Brennan Center for Justice. n.d. *Social & Economic Harm.* Accessed July 20, 2024. https://www.brennancenter.org/issues/end-mass-incarceration/social-economic-harm.

Carruthers, William. 2023. *How Egypt's Aswan Dam Washed Away Nubian Heritage.* February 24. https://newlinesmag.com/essays/how-egypts-aswan-dam-washed-away-nubian-heritage/#:~:text=Over%20the%20course%20of%20the,the%20Egypt-ian%20city%20of%20Aswan.

Debusmann, Jr., Bernd. 2023. "Why Do So Many Police Traffice Stops Turn Deadly?" *BBC.* January 31. https://www.bbc.com/news/world-us-canada-64458041.

Farlex, Inc. . n.d. *The Free Dictionary by Farlex, Inc. .* Feasterville, PA.

Festinger, Leon. 1962. *A Theory of Cognitive Dissonance.* Redwood: Standford University Press.

Friedman, Jonathan, and Nadine Johnson. 2022. "Banned in the USA: Rising School Book Bans Threaten Free Expression and Students' First Amendment Rights ." *PEN America.* April. https://pen.org/banned-in-the-usa/#trends.

Gauthier, Lane Roy; Lousiana State University and Agricultural & Mechanical College. 1982. "A Study of the Three-Level Hierarchy of Information Processing in Reading Comprehension with Respect to Cognitive Demand." *LSU Historical Dissertations and Theses.* Baton Rouge, Louisiana: LSU Scholarly Repository.

Grall, Timothy. 2020. *Custodial Mothers and Fathers .* U.S. Census bureau.

Haslanger, Sally. n.d. "Ancient Philosophy."

Homans, Charles, interview by Terry Gross. 2022. *Journalist* (July 28).

Horowitz, Juliana Menasce, Anna Brown, and Kiana Cox. 2019. "Race in America 2019." *Pew Research Center.* April 9. Accessed July 7, 2024. https://www.pewresearch.org/social-trends/2019/04/09/race-in-america-2019/.

James, George G.M. 1954. *Stolen Legacy.* General Press.

Kamisar, Ben. 2023. *Almost a third of Americans still believe the 2020 election result was fraudulent.* June 20. Accessed 2023. https://www.nbcnews.com/meet-the-press/meetthepressblog/almost-third-americans-still-believe-2020-election-result-was-fraudule-rcna90145.

Pedrazas, David. 2021. "National Child Custody Statistics by Gender." *Law Offices of David Pedrazas, PLLC.* July 8. Accessed July 8, 2024. https://utahdivorce.biz/national-child-custody-statistics-by-gender/.

Samuelson, Kristin. 2023. *Americans' IQ scores are lower in some areas, higher in one.* March 20. https://news.northwestern.edu/stories/2023/03/americans-iq-scores-are-lower-in-some-areas-higher-in-one/#:~:text=IQ%20scores%20have%20substantially%20increased,as%20the%20%E2%80%9CFlynn%20effect.%E2%80%9D.

Stephens, James. 2010. *The Slavery of the British West India Colonies Delineated: As it Exists Both in Law and Practice, and Compared with the Slavery of Other Countries, Ancient and Modern.* Cambridge: Cambridge University PRess.

Substance Abuse and Mental Health Services Administration. 2016. *2015 National Survey on Drug Use and Health.* Rockville, MD: Substance Abuse and Mental Health Services Administration.

The British Museum. 2017. "Everything you ever wanted to know about the Rosetta Stone." *The British Museum.* July 14. Accessed June 30, 2024. https://www.british-museum.org/blog/everything-you-ever-wanted-know-about-rosetta-stone.

The National Association for the Advancement of Colored People. n.d. "Criminal Justice Fact Sheet." *NAACP.* Accessed July 6, 2024. https://naacp.org/resources/criminal-justice-fact-sheet.

—. n.d. "The Origins of Modern Day Policing." *NAACP.* Accessed July 6, 2024. https://naacp.org/find-resources/history-explained/origins-modern-day-policing.

The National Library of Medicine| The National Center for Biotechnology Information. 2009. "Characterizing the admixed African ancestry of African Americans." *The National Library of Medicine| The National Center for Biotechnology Information.* https://www.ncbi.nlm.nih.gov/pmc/articles/PMC2812948/.

The National Urban League. 2019. *The National Urban League.* https://78ab0743.flowpaper.com/NULSOBA2024ExecutiveSummary-web/#page=1.

United States Sentencing Commission. 2023. "Demographic Differences in Federal Sentencing." *United States Sentencing Commission.* November. Accessed July 9, 2024. https://www.ussc.gov/sites/default/files/pdf/research-and-publications/research-publications/2023/20231114_Demographic-Differences.pdf.

White, Evelyn. 1914. "Hesiod, Homeric Hymns, Epic Cycle." *H G. Loeb Classical Library Volume 57.*

Windsor, Malik. 2022. *The Importance of Black Literature.* December 5. https://centerforblackliterature.org/the-importance-of-black-litera-ture/#:~:text=Their%20work%20provided%20white%20America,inequality%2C%20discrimination%2C%20and%20stereotype.

York, Malachi Z. n.d. *What is Nuwau-Bu?* Eatonton, Georgia: The Holy Tabernacle Ministries.